Do Story

How to tell your story
so the world listens

Bobette Buster

BooK Co

Published by
The Do Book Company 2013
Works in Progress Publishing Ltd
thedobook.co

This edition published 2018

Text © Bobette Buster 2013, 2018
Illustrations © Millie Marotta 2013

The right of Bobette Buster to be
identified as the author of this work
has been asserted by her in accordance
with the Copyright, Designs and Patents
Act 1988

In certain case studies names have been
changed to respect the identities of
those concerned

A CIP catalogue record for this book is
available from the British Library

ISBN 978-1-907974-46-5

10 9 8 7 6 5 4

To find out more about our company,
books and authors, please visit
thedobook.co or follow us **@dobookco**

5% of our proceeds from the sale of this
book is given to the Do Lectures to help
it achieve its aim of making positive
change **thedolectures.com**

Cover designed by James Victore
Book designed and typeset by Ratiotype

Printed and bound by OZGraf Print
on Munken, an FSC® certified paper

'Were it not for the storyteller,
civilisation would destroy itself.'

—

Albert Camus

To my father, Robert, the greatest storyteller
I have ever known.

And to my mother, Shirley, the greatest listener
– and laugher, along with my brothers, three.
Chief among my memories is us all gathered
around the table, hoping the long evenings
of storytelling would never end.

And for me, they never did.

Contents

'Carry the fire.'

—

Cormac McCarthy

Introduction

Stories are the fire we carry to each other. In Cormac McCarthy's novel *No Country for Old Men*, Sheriff Bell recalls that his cowboy father would carry the embers from the fire of one camp to the next in an animal horn. It was a tradition passed to the cowboys by the Native American Indians. In the novel, this important act had another meaning: to have hope and continue the quest, but also to maintain humanity. The fire carrier would hold a special position in the tribe and for their society.

Stories possess a spark, a power: to comfort, connect, destroy, transform – and even to heal. Everyone has a story to tell. And everyone can appreciate a great story well told. But we are not all gifted storytellers. However, in all my years of teaching 'The Art of Storytelling' around the world, I have never known anyone to fail at learning how to tell their story, beautifully, once they learned what you will discover in this book. Storytelling, as you will see, is elemental within each of us.

The very act of telling your story possesses power. It is through the act of telling and hearing stories that we become inspired. We can envisage a better life for ourselves. The end result is, in fact, that we become courageous. Then, a curious thing happens. Our actions – our individual act of courage – are what lead to 'healing in the land', that is, the transformation of our world.

Equally powerful is the inverse. The power of storytelling can be lethal. The fact is, history has shown us that stories not told can become like an evil genie left in a bottle.

When they are finally uncorked, their power to destroy is unleashed.

Consider the case in the US, on 5 November 2011, when it was revealed that one of the US's most revered college football coaches, Joe Paterno of Pennsylvania State University (known as Penn State), had withheld vital information for over 14 years – that his assistant coach, Jerry Sandusky, had been accused of 40 cases of child sex abuse. Joe, known as 'JoePa', was possibly the most beloved football coach in US history. But he simply didn't possess the courage to tell the truth. He could not face the reality of the 'story' he was in. When it finally came out, Joe Paterno was summarily fired, causing students to riot in support of him. He died six weeks later from lung cancer. Jerry Sandusky was tried and found guilty.

Equally, stories can destroy with their gossip, innuendo, and character defamation.

The demise of Rupert Murdoch's *News of the World* was at long last achieved when both the public and the UK government could no longer tolerate the newspaper management's blatant disregard for a grieving family's privacy. Yet their long reign of power was largely due to the public's mob-like appetite for the story, no matter how dubiously it had been obtained.

This book will not be about these sensationalist stories, or tellers.

Rather, this book is about the power of stories to heal, to restore, to share a vision and, most of all, to inspire others. This will be the stuff of the stories you will read in the ensuing chapters – and all of them are personal and true. You'll hear about charity entrepreneurs driven by the fact that they could 'no longer afford the luxury of their ignorance', about citizen diplomats, community activists, and a cast-off politician who saved the world.

You will discover the power of alchemy as we enter worlds we would otherwise never know in Copenhagen, Uganda, a suburb of Paris and a small town in Kentucky.

As I share these stories with you, I will encourage you to notice certain elements or shared characteristics that turn them from good to great. And it is these elements that, I hope, you will start to display in your own storytelling.

All we have had from our caveman campfire days until relatively recently (in historical terms) was the oral tradition. The wisdom of the ages has been handed down by the shamans, medicine men, or griots from tribal cultures the world over via folklore, fairytales, myths and legends. This is how each generation was psychologically prepared for their future – to be ready, to know that they would not only be able to survive, but that they would thrive amid life's inevitable adversities.

It has been said that the Industrial Age ended after World War Two. Then, it was superseded by the Age of Information via the computer, the 1960s boom in Madison Avenue advertising (see the hit show *Mad Men*) and television. Then with the Internet boom of the 1990s, there followed in 2003 the viral explosion of social media. With it a new deceiving conceit arose: that anything worth knowing is available at our fingertips. This immediacy has, curiously, made people less curious about discovering the world, at least in any depth. Now, with 24/7 news cycles, hours spent tweeting or updating Facebook pages with daily minutia, and endless reality television shows, the full power of storytelling – its contextual beauty and majestic ability to move us – is on the wane.

What this means is that today's children may know the facts but not the context in which things happen. As they are no longer being shaped by a storytelling world, they seem to lack the will to dig deeper, preferring to surf in the immediate.

I was struck by this recently when a graduate from one of America's most elite schools asked me, 'Was John Lennon in that group ... don't tell me ... Wings?'

Or when a student at France's top film programme, La Fémis, asked me offhandedly, 'What was it that Jean-Luc Godard did that was so great?'

Or when I overheard a Detroit mother of three share a major revelation, without irony, 'I just found out that George Washington was the Father of Our Country. I always wondered who that man was on the quarter.' This, despite the fact that every year on the third Monday of February, the US has a national holiday to celebrate President's Day in honour of Washington's (and Lincoln's) birthdays. When I was in school – and I daresay for the previous 200 years – on 22 February of each year, every school child learned the story of George Washington, that when he was a boy, he freely confessed to his father, 'I cannot tell a lie. I chopped down that cherry tree.' This story was like the air we breathed.

A recent ground-breaking study for children, 'Do You Know?' (created by psychologist Dr Marshall Duke of Emory University and his colleague, Dr Robyn Fivush) has discovered the single best predictor of children's emotional health and happiness: Story. Apparently, the more a child knows his family's 'story' – in other words, the better informed he is about his wider family and obstacles they have overcome in order to survive and thrive – the 'stronger a child's sense of control over his life, the higher his self-esteem'.

The issue is getting parents to sit down with their children and tell them their stories. Perhaps they never sat down with their own parents long enough to learn theirs.

However, all is not lost. It would appear that we are now entering a new age: the Age of Story (back to the campfire!), or rather, the era of Content Creation. That is, whoever owns the best story will win. So it is vital that we each learn to tell our story well, so that our stories become the best they can be. But first, we must respect the fact that no story can succeed without a proper understanding of 'context', that is the proper set-up of the story in order to frame its wisdom and clarify its emotions.

Norman Lear, creator of *All in the Family* (one of the most revered television series in US history), said, 'We live in the most emotionally cluttered time in history.' Stories provide clarity. They help us to know how to feel and how to understand the world around us. Without this context, the next generation will be rudderless and confused. So, yes, there is absolute power in mastering this.

I hope that this book will provide you with the tools you need to tell your own story with passion and resonance. That you will be able to cajole, persuade, mesmerise your listener with vivid imagery and be able to create lasting emotional connections.

Within each of the chapters that follow, I present a central story, occasionally supported by smaller stories. Each will illustrate a key point as to the 'how' of storytelling. My intent is that each chapter will clarify a point, while building on it, much like a pyramid. You will also be able to observe one fundamental, immutable fact about storytelling, that Aristotle was right: all good stories possess structure. They have a beginning, middle and end.

Right at the end of the book are a few exercises so you can practise your new storytelling skills before you tackle that big presentation or write your company's back story, or simply carry the fire of your own story forward.

'I keep six honest serving men
(They taught me all I knew);
Their names are What and Why and When
And How and Where and Who.'

—

Rudyard Kipling, *The Elephant's Child*

1
The Craft

Kipling, that great master of storytelling if ever there was one, understood that stories must have a basic structure and answer the fundamental questions: who, what, when, where, why, how. This framework is drunk like mother's milk by all news reporters from day one of their coverage of any story they tell. As Sgt Joe Friday would say in his deadpan voice in the hit US crime show *Dragnet*: 'Just gimme the facts, ma'am. Just the facts.' However, Kipling also knew that it is what lies behind these facts that creates the emotional connection. And that is key to great storytelling. Or, as I call it, the story behind the story.

But first, a bit about listening. As Ralph Waldo Emerson, the renowned 19th-century transcendentalist poet, astutely observed, people are always telling you what they really think whether they know it or not. If you are listening, you will observe this. We are always broadcasting our own inner thoughts revealed by asides, our attitude, our point of view volunteered in an offhand manner. This is why mastering the art of storytelling is essential. It will give you the discipline of knowing what not to say – or give away – as much as what to say.

During my 20 years of teaching, I have been primarily listening. I tend to start each new session by having my students simply tell me – and the assembled group – something about themselves we would otherwise never know. The first two or three students usually share some simple fact about their life. Nothing that reveals too much about themselves. They laugh, nervous, embarrassed – as do their peers. Everyone shares in their discomfort. Meanwhile, what I am doing is listening. I observe just how nervous or diffident they are. I ask myself, 'Why have they chosen this particular era of their life for the story they are telling now?' And then I listen to what they're not saying to try and find the real story.

I tend to interrupt with just one or two questions. Thereafter, they will, without fail, tell us the actual story. From that point onwards, everyone in the entire room anxiously awaits their turn. All the students' stories become deeper and more profound. Each person, you see, wants to be heard. We all have a story we want to tell.

For example, in one class, a male student blithely discussed an 'interesting trip' he took to Israel after his marriage broke up. He gave an almost blasé account of his visit to Jerusalem and the West Bank. When he finished I asked him, 'Why did you choose to go to Israel so soon after your divorce?' The room hushed. He blinked back tears, and replied, yes, his marriage had broken up after 15 years. He then reflected that the trip had actually been a kind of spiritual quest for him.

I tell my students that I am not attempting to pry, nor create a kind of New Age Californian group bonding moment. No, rather I am simply listening for the 'threshold' moment. We all arrive at thresholds. The question is: what do we do at that moment? Do we freeze, grow numb, or try to run away? Or do we face our fear, and gather the courage to go through the 'refining fire'?

Another student, a handsome young man in his late twenties, volunteered that he had been a football player in the major league until he was hurt in a game. He couldn't continue due to his injury. Everyone in the room gasped, delighted. What an exciting fact. Someone in our midst had been a 'star' – well, an orbiting minor star in a major constellation. Meanwhile I was observing his body language, how he looked into the distance as he spoke. At the end I merely asked, 'What was it like, letting go of that life, a game you'd played since you were a small boy?' Again, tears sprang up in his eyes. He said quietly, 'I got to play ... I got to play in the Big League ...' He could say no more but his years of hard work and shattered dreams were suddenly vividly present.

Then there was the female student, a lovely Sri Lankan, Maya, who was urgently waiting for me after my class in Ronda, Spain. She had taken my class a year earlier, which ended on 15 December 2004. The next day, she had flown back to her country for the Christmas break. On 26 December, she and two friends had driven their scooters to the beach and were walking across an isthmus to the island offshore when they heard an overpowering, deafening roar. From both sides, the great tsunami was racing towards their sliver of land, swallowing everything in its path. They tried to run. But the mountainous waves – from both sides – rose up to snatch them. All three clung to each other. Maya said that at that moment, she recalled the life lesson I had just taught her from the wisdom of storytelling: that we must all learn to recognise the power of the meta-narrative being played out in our lives, and that at some key moment we will be called upon to 'let go' and allow ourselves to be transformed. Somehow, as Maya released her will, at that moment she was lifted up and carried all the way back inland, along with her two friends. When the water receded they were surrounded by destruction, debris and death. And they were left in awe, deeply humbled.

The purpose of my questions is never to lead people into a moment of public group therapy. My intention is always to encourage people to see their own part in the grand narrative that is currently being played out in their lives.

Because we are all in the midst of a great story. There is a continual narrative at work, inexorably being shaped and honed by our life choices. Storytelling provides the lens through which we can see those choices more clearly. It gives us perspective. With this clarity, we can then seize our destiny. We are not victims being tossed haplessly to and fro. We can appreciate the choices we need to make with objective eyes; we can vent our frustrations; sort out our confusions; untangle a web of lies even. All so that we can find our way to a much larger story. One that we control consciously now, with our eyes wide open. Through stories our true character is revealed, or transformed in the process, like the refining away of the dross in order to make gold.

Growing up, I was fortunate. I got to listen to many of the great storytellers from where I was born. In fact, I descend from a long line of them. My forefather, a Revolutionary War patriot (who fought with George Washington at Valley Forge), settled in Kentucky as, after the war, all soldiers were given land grants. That's where our farm was founded, on an elevated plain once used by the Cherokee Indians (we uncovered their pots beneath the house, along with thousands of Indian arrowhead tips). Twenty other families settled in this rugged, hilly terrain flowing out of the Appalachian mountain range. This became the rural aristocratic community known as Creelsboro. The town itself was only accessible by steamboat, dry creek beds or the buffalo trails – ancient wide paths cutting through dense forest. When my forefathers came, they brought with them slaves to fell the ancient thousand-year-old trees. Sometime early on, long before the US Civil War, those slaves were freed and given parcels of land up in the hollows above our farm.

When I was in my twenties, in the late 1970s, I obtained a small financial grant to collect the oral history of this remote Brigadoon-like valley where the same community of families had lived for over 150 years. I wanted to capture the stories of my elders before they passed on.

I could only find one African–American woman, Luella, who had descended from my family's slaves. Luella told a lot of stories about growing up in Creelsboro, including how her 94-year-old grandmother recalled seeing the last Cherokee tribe leave our little valley. They moved off in the foggy river mist, taking the buffalo trail, never to be seen again. Then, I asked her, what was it like growing up in this remote, inaccessible river valley? Luella knew what I was really asking her. The question that I didn't have the courage to ask: 'What was it like being black in an all-white community?' Luella pulled her shoulders back, clasped her hands in her lap with full dignity and said, 'I'll tell you one thing. I did not know I was coloured until I moved away.'

That's when I understood that my family had been pioneering abolitionists. When I asked my great-aunt Margie, born in 1898, about this, she was offended: 'Why, we would never draw attention to our actions or politics. That's just the way things were. Everyone was equal in Creelsboro.'

I would never have known this if I had not hunted down the story.

I got the research grant because the US Library of Congress had recognised that a whole native American art form was about to die: oral history. So they issued a Call for Grants. In my quest to capture these soon-to-be-lost memories, I awakened to something quite new. I found myself on a kind of fantastic journey in time-travel, carried by the lyricisms, witticisms and cadences of expert storytellers, all honed in the remote Appalachian hillsides, like diamonds found in coal. I became filled with pride about my heritage and I came to see that storytelling was the very glue of life. In my family's small town, you had to tell one every day. It was more than a matter of conversation. Stories were the primary form of entertainment. It was the iPod and social networking tool of its era. People wanted to tell the best story. And so, in this rough terrain of constant pressure of 'one up', great diamonds were formed.

I can see now that storytelling was ubiquitous. It came from my grandparents, aunts, uncles, father, neighbours, pastors, shopkeepers around the town square. When anyone arrived, a piece of pie would be offered, fresh coffee put on. And then the stories would begin. One would lead to another. 'That reminds me of the time ...' someone would say. When I was very little, as the evening advanced, I would be sent upstairs to bed. My mother would often find me, hours later, asleep at the bottom of the staircase, my head against the crack in the door. I'd been listening for as long as my weary head could hold up.

And so years later, I wandered for two years throughout the region on a kind of pilgrimage, collecting the stories of an age vanishing before my eyes. After I'd given my audiotapes to the Kentucky Museum archives, I made my way to Hollywood and their inner sanctum: the very realm of cinema story development. It was here that I found my tribe. Soon I realised the 'business of show business' is entirely based on how well you tell your story. I have to admit that, at first, I was flummoxed. Why was this so hard? Then, I realised I had to deconstruct something I took for granted in order to teach others how well this could be done.

In doing so, I discovered several fundamental principles of storytelling and have since crafted these into a list of ten that I return to time and again.

These principles appear on the next page. We will explore all of them in the following chapters. Trust the process; it will become second nature because storytelling is, after all, what we have been born to do.

The 10 Principles of Storytelling

1. Tell your story as if you're telling it to a friend: this applies no matter where you are or who your audience is.

2. Set the GPS: give the place, time, setting, and any relevant context. Keep it factual, short and sweet.

3. Action! Use active verbs or, as I like to say, 'Think Hemingway': spice up your verb choices but keep them succinct. Invest in a thesaurus (or a free app). Avoid multisyllabic, erudite, four-dollar words, over-intellectualising, philosophising, qualifying. See how many I just used? It's boring to keep reading them, isn't it?

4. Juxtapose: take two ideas, images, or thoughts and place them together. Let them collide. Remember German philosopher, Friedrich Hegel, here: that in posing two opposing ideas, a whole new idea is created (thesis + antithesis = synthesis). This tool wakes up your audience, and is the root of all successful stories.

5. Gleaming detail: choose one ordinary moment or object that becomes a 'gleaming detail'. Something that best captures and embodies the essence of the story. Make the ordinary extraordinary.

6. 'Hand over the Spark': reflect on the experience or idea that originally captivated you and simply hand it to your audience as if it were aflame. Carry the fire.

7. Be vulnerable: dare to share the emotion of your story. Be unafraid to ask your audience what you questioned along the way so they share your doubt, confusion, anger, sorrow, insight, glee, delight, joy, epiphany.

8. Tune in to your sense memory: choose the strongest of the five senses in your story and use it to make a deeper connection with your audience. There is always one primary sense that dominates every memory.

9. Bring yourself: a story is as much about you as anything else.

10. Let go: hand over your story, letting it build to its natural, emotional punchline, then end it and get out fast. Leave the audience wanting more. Less is more.

'You can speak well if you …
can deliver the message of your heart.'

John Ford

2
The Tools

Some time ago, a young American woman, DJ Forza, approached me to ask for advice. She had recently been invited to give a TEDx talk in Zug, Switzerland. She had been asked to share the journey of how she came to undertake a PhD in Citizen Diplomacy. As delighted as DJ was to have this opportunity, she was equally, like so many, terrified of the prospect of public speaking. In the course of our discussions, I witnessed DJ take another journey – to becoming a confident and successful storyteller. She did so by employing all ten of my principles of storytelling. I will share with you now our process. In so doing, I hope you will begin to recognise the tools you will need to source, structure and shape your own stories.

The afternoon that DJ and I met, we were facing the 'uncertain glory of an April day' (to quote Shakespeare). I suggested we take a walk in the misty rain through a bluebell dell. Walking is good for this sort of discussion because it helps to generate a different flow of ideas – as opposed to sitting face to face like a patient and therapist. But essentially, the beautiful setting and the physical exercise helped dissipate DJ's fear about talking to me, the supposed expert. I simply listened to her – as a friend. DJ's main anxiety about her upcoming 20-minute talk was far from uncommon: she felt she had too much to express in too little time, and she didn't know how to 'tame the beast'. Hers was a large, noble subject and she desperately wanted to inspire her listeners, as she had been inspired, to consider contributing their personal vacation time to volunteering in the world's worst crisis areas.

I asked DJ specific, focused questions. What had been her personal journey? She revealed, reluctantly, that she had been a successful corporate executive based in NYC. She resisted discussing this at first. She didn't want to call attention to herself. She continued on about how much she wanted to share: how people in poverty or war-torn places do not want a 'hand out', they want a 'hand up' to help them get on their way. She continued to emphasise, with passion but in general terms, how well organised the international relief organisations were with whom she had volunteered. She talked about how some people can let their compassion get the better of them when they see a disaster on the news. They show up to help but, effectively, they are tourists. In a disaster there's no time for that, and hence they exhaust the resources of the recovery effort.

This was all well and good information but it was verging on the boring, so I stopped her. I wanted to hear her personal story. By bringing herself into the story, I knew this would encourage the audience to connect with her. I asked: what were her struggles? What had she taken away from all these experiences?

But DJ did not want to go there. She believed no one would be interested. Or even should be. It was the content of her mission that was more important. To speak about herself would diminish the importance of the work.

So I tried a different tack: I asked her, 'What is the

first memory that comes to mind when you think of your various volunteer efforts anywhere in the world?'

Immediately, DJ became emotional. Her voice softened. She brushed away the tears. She recalled 11 March 2011, the day of the devastating Japanese earthquake, then tsunami, followed by the subsequent nuclear plant meltdown.

Due to her on-going contacts with an organised volunteer corps, DJ was able to fly out soon after to Japan as part of the massive global clean-up effort in the tragedy's aftermath. For days on end, DJ and her team of international volunteers worked side by side with the Japanese families whose homes, and entire towns, had been swept into unrecognisable shattered heaps. Hundreds of locals laboured alongside the volunteers. During those endless, numbing hours of sorting and cleaning up, DJ noticed a middle-aged Japanese woman working alongside a very elderly Japanese couple. She was their daughter, and spoke English, whereas they did not.

After several long days, the daughter asked DJ if she would come to their home for tea. DJ was immediately taken aback by this invitation. It was such an honour. She accepted and went to their home, which was still only partially intact after the disaster. While the elderly Japanese mother carefully prepared the tea, DJ looked around the room. Along one wall were a number of World War Two-era photographs of a handsome young Japanese soldier, presumably the elderly man with whom she was about to take tea, and who was sitting quietly in the corner, observing her every move. DJ quietly asked the daughter if this young soldier was her father. 'Yes,' she replied, 'they are all photos of my father during the war.' The elderly couple noticed that DJ was looking at the photos. They remained silent. Then the daughter said,

'This is why my mother wanted to make tea for you. She could not believe that an American would come all this way to help us. She wanted to personally thank you.'

I told her that she had to tell this story but DJ was afraid that she would break down in tears if she did.

But this was the real story, or 'the story behind the story' (more on this later). It was the single event that inspired DJ to understand the importance of Citizen Diplomacy. It inspired her to leave her successful corporate career in New York and become a Kiva fellow (an international programme that selects qualified professionals to work as unpaid volunteers in support of global microfinance in over 60 countries around the world). DJ lived for five months in Tbilisi, Georgia, the former Soviet state. From these experiences, she is now doing a PhD in Citizen Diplomacy in Geneva.

Naturally, I encouraged DJ to try to tell this story – because in the specific story, you tell the universal. Sure, she would risk breaking down for a moment, but I assured her that we should never forget that our audience longs to be moved. We all long to connect. That is all.

A couple of months later DJ gave her talk. She opened with a brilliant juxtaposition. She said, 'What if you told your mother you were spending your vacation in the worst, most poverty-stricken, wretched part of the world?' I thought that was an excellent 'lead'. She hooked her audience right away with two colliding ideas that would wake them up. In this case, it was: your vacation time versus your call to help others. DJ was then able to weave the story of her own personal journey throughout her belief in the power of Citizen Diplomacy. She described the on-going efforts around the world to provide well-organised, trained volunteer networks that can land within days of a disaster and provide welcome relief.

She showed before and after images of the clean-up efforts in Japan, of post-earthquake Haiti, and of poverty in war-torn areas around the world.

After her talk, DJ told me that many people in the audience came up to personally thank her for telling her story. They had been deeply moved, and could even see themselves learning how to become a professional volunteer. This had been DJ's objective all along.

I was moved, too. This is the pure joy of storytelling. To enlighten your audience and, ideally, move them to take action. An action that will improve the world. You cannot ask for more.

Full disclosure: in the end, DJ could not bring herself to tell the story of her involvement with the Japanese tsunami. She was still too afraid that she would break down. So, with her permission, I'm telling it here – for her.

So, let's analyse DJ's process in learning how to tell her story. Before her talk:

1. She was afraid and nervous. Note: we all are. Even Ringo Starr (a Beatle, for God's sake!) confesses that he still feels sick before going on stage, to this day.

2. She felt she had too much to tell in too little time. This is always the problem. How do we 'tame the beast' and source those key elements that will make the most compelling story?

3. She didn't want to draw attention to herself when her objective was much bigger than she was.

4. She was afraid of becoming emotional in public.

5. She felt the burden of wanting to impart the importance of her subject: the power of Citizen Diplomacy. She felt it was her responsibility to get it right.

Here are the practical steps she took when crafting her story:

1. She hooked in her audience early on by juxtaposing two colliding ideas: taking a holiday and going to one of the most wretched, poverty-stricken places on the planet. It was a headline that was visual and active. Imagine a terrible place. Imagine going there on your vacation. This was her lead.

2. She took the audience on a journey. She made it personal so that they could follow her.

3. She demonstrated where her dream of Citizen Diplomacy came from and then the struggle or issues around this idea. Specifically, DJ wanted to communicate that it's important to not be a 'compassion tourist', but rather to volunteer with a reputable organisation experienced in disaster relief.

4. She appealed to at least one sense: the visual. She made sure to show specific images of disaster areas, both the horror of the disaster, and then the aftermath. When her audience could see the overwhelming need for 'all hands on deck' after the Japanese tsunami, they could then appreciate the same sight months later, partially cleared up.

5.   Her own actions as a volunteer ennobled her audience in the telling. At her story's end, they were inspired to take action, too.

In my retelling of DJ's story, I also provided a 'little thing' or the 'gleaming detail' of a simple Japanese tea. By being invited to partake in the ordinary, DJ experienced an extraordinary thing: the power of Citizen Diplomacy to heal – across decades and thousands of miles.

Read on as we discuss the power of the gleaming detail in greater depth.

'It's the little things.'

—

Vincent Vega, *Pulp Fiction*

3
The Gleaming Detail

To make a story unforgettable, you need to find that one image that connects with the audience, that 'Aha!' moment. This creates the epiphany we seek in a great story – that surprise revelation or sigh of recognition. This singular image, well positioned, can elevate a story from good ... to great. We call this the 'gleaming detail' – a term originally derived from that great nation of storytellers, the Irish – for the element that makes a story stand out.

The gleaming detail is the one thing that captures both the emotion and idea of the story at once, in one fell swoop. A singular, elegant moment of clarity. It is a literal representation of the truth that is inherent within every story. So as you develop your story, ask yourself: what is the truth within the story that I want to tell?

Working this way, your story's own unique gleaming detail may well present itself. First of all, listen to what the story is telling you. Usually, the essence of the story will reveal itself in an ordinary detail. Think back to DJ Forza and the simple act of sharing tea. Go with this. Don't overthink it. Quite often the more ordinary the detail, the greater or more 'extraordinary' the truth that is revealed.

To give you an example, a student of mine from Denmark told my class the story of her grandmother Helga, her father's mother.

In the late 1940s, Helga went to court to appeal for a divorce on the grounds of 'intolerable cruelty'. This was at a time when no woman dared to divorce her husband. Risking her financial future was not advisable for a woman.

Helga and her husband were well-respected members of a Catholic community. They had two young sons, aged three and five, and lived in a fine home. They were prosperous. However, events drove Helga to appeal for divorce. She was forced to plead her own case to the judge because no lawyer wanted to be associated with a woman. In the end, the judge did grant Helga a divorce, but not before he took the opportunity to publicly berate her, asserting that her commitment to this course of action revealed her poor character. She must be a weak wife, an extremely disappointing example of a mother. He pitied her sons and, purely to grant them stability, he awarded Helga the home. When Helga finally left the court and returned to the house, she opened the door and found it entirely empty. While she had been at court all day (being humiliated by the judge), every single item had been removed: all the furniture, the wardrobes full of clothes, the beds, the children's toys, the lights. Even the light sockets had been ripped out of the walls.

In this brief story, universal in its heartache, we are given one 'gleaming detail' that shows us what might have motivated this woman to endure the public humiliation of a divorce. With the image of the ripped-out light sockets, we can fully understand her desperate need to separate herself from a petty, vindictive man who would deny his own children not only their toys, but electricity – light and warmth. This ordinary detail explains the story's hidden truth: Helga's emotional despair. The image of ripped-out light sockets shows us how extraordinarily heartless her home had become. We are moved to compassion for her, and now feel admiration for her courage.

Notice that I set up the story with a brief headline: a woman's appeal for divorce in the 1940s when it was unusual, and a huge financial risk. You, the audience, are given the simplest of facts. There is no judgement about her husband. In the first instance, no reasons are given for her course of action. All we are told is that Helga put herself out on a limb and, in doing so, endured a public harangue from the judge. As the story continues we follow Helga home and discover that everything that could make a home habitable is gone – their clothes, furniture, even the children's toys. When it comes to the light fixtures we are left asking, who would take the time to rip light sockets out?

Today, part of the problem is that we have had our emotional radar dulled. We are less sensitive to the smaller details and feel we have to spoon-feed our audience. To fill in the blanks for them. Many storytellers think it impressive to qualify tales with flowery adverbs or politically correct statements. Consider this retelling of the same story: 'Now this will be a terribly hard experience for you to imagine, but this is the story of a woman whose husband was bitterly vindictive and made her home life so difficult she was driven to desperate measures.' And then we might have ended the story with, 'That goes to show just how mean a husband and father he was that the first priority for his wife, now destitute, would be to source and pay for an expensive electrician,' and so on.

You don't need to do this. Don't qualify, justify or explain. Simply tell the story. And leave the emotional impact to resound as it no doubt will. The key here is to use the gleaming detail as a device, and to use it sparingly.

It should never dominate or become obvious as a storytelling device. Be economical with it. Position it only once or twice so that it will stand out.

Here is a classic film illustration of how the ordinary becomes extraordinary. In Steven Spielberg's much-loved film *ET* (Universal Pictures, 1982), we are given a brilliant gleaming detail. The most ordinary of objects in a ten-year-old boy's life: a bicycle.

Most of us have seen the film, and probably more than once, so you will recall how it opens with space aliens gathering specimens in a redwood forest on a remote hilltop, overlooking a US cityscape below. It is night time and the city lights shine brightly. All of a sudden, the aliens are frightened and make a hasty departure, launching their spaceship into the night sky. However, one small alien is accidentally left behind. All alone in the forest.

The next day Elliott, a ten-year-old boy, arrives in the forest on his bicycle. He is exploring, also alone. We don't think anything about his bicycle, an ordinary, everyday object for a child. Later that day, we learn that Elliott's father has recently left his family, and is now in Mexico with another woman. We also discover that Elliott is the younger brother of 16-year-old Michael who, along with his three friends, loves to taunt him. So Elliott is very lonely. That evening, the older boys won't even let Elliott play their board game. They make him go outside in the dark to get their pizza. He's afraid and, sure enough, he hears a scary noise. The noise leads him to discover ET behind their house. They both scream in fright. But then the next day, Elliott gets on his bicycle and, alone, goes back into the forest near his home. Walking alongside his bicycle, he tosses candy out onto the woodland floor, creating a trail back to his home, in the hope that ET will follow it. We don't think anything about Elliott using his bicycle, this being the most ordinary mode of transport, and self-reliance, for a ten-year-old. The next day, Elliott opens his back door, and is astonished to find ET handing back the candy. Leading his new alien friend safely inside, Elliott creates a cosy den for ET in his closet. The next day, Elliott tries to tell his brother and the other boys about his alien friend while sitting on his bicycle as they are getting on the school bus. Of course, they tease him unmercifully. They board the school bus laughing at him.

Thereafter, Elliott continues getting to know ET, on his own. They form a kind of mystical friendship. Finally, ET reveals to Elliott his plan to 'phone home' – just as the US authorities figure out his whereabouts. The balance shifts as Michael and his buddies accept that Elliott does indeed possess 'power'. When the police cars arrive, Michael and his three friends jump on their bicycles and lead the police on a merry race through suburban backyards, even leaping off the police car roofs. They manage to get away. The bicycles win!

Once they have outwitted the police, the boys ride to the park where they discover Elliott with ET, the little alien sitting in the bicycle basket draped in a white sheet. They are awestruck. The balance has shifted: Elliott is the leader of the pack. The boys fall in behind him on their bicycles, racing through the streets in order to get to the forest in time to meet the mother ship. While they are riding, a man steps out and holds a gun towards Elliott. In extreme close-up, Elliott closes his eyes in terror. Then ... the ordinary becomes the extraordinary. Literally. The bicycles leave the ground and lift up high towards the mountain. What follows is one of the most magical moments in film history as the boys on their bicycles fly in front of a full moon. When they reach the forest, Elliott – in the lead –

demonstrates to the four 16-year-olds following him how to land in unison, as one. There, aglow in the darkness of the forest, awaits the spaceship, poised to take off.

Elliott watches his best friend, ET, depart. He stands nobly apart from his mother, brother and sister. We know that he will never be lonely again, because someone 'out there' will always love him unconditionally.

The boy's bicycle is a perfect use of an ordinary object that becomes extraordinary. This singular act of the bikes crossing the moon represents the full emotional arc of Elliott's transformation into a self-reliant young man. His coming of age.

Stories provide the context to understand the awakening of transformation. The call to conscience, the blooming of the soul into maturity. This experience is at its most powerful when it occurs at the cusp of an era, a transitional turning point in a person's life, or in current events, as we experience the world change before our very eyes. So how do we get *that* across in a story?

'I think it is the excitement
only a free man can feel.
A free man at the start of
a long journey whose
conclusion is uncertain.'

—

Red, *The Shawshank Redemption*

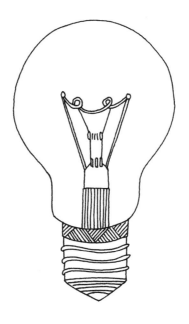

'I met a man once who said that they "didn't have any fire", and he had to go to Mr Somebody's house and "borry some fire". Well those words just hit me. They were electrical ... something elemental about life.'

—

Eudora Welty, author

4
Hand Over the Spark

Stories are always about transformation. Whether we know it or not, whatever the story we are telling, we are always sharing a 'threshold' moment. This means that we are at a crossroads in our life, a turning point, a fork in the road. This threshold is a call for us to wake up, or to rise to a challenge before us. Fundamentally, we are being called to change. To discover the courage to become our best selves. This moment is always 'elemental' – a kind of fire, a spark carrying us towards transformation.

For so many of us our personal story is hinged on a particular moment that caused us to completely change our lives and the direction in which we were heading, whether in our personal or professional lives. For many, this transformative moment became the starting point for our life's work.

So how do we 'hand over this spark' when sharing our story – either in person or via our company website, for example – so the audience feels what we felt at that defining moment?

Charities and non-profits who perform acts of goodwill often 'preach' their story in an attempt to get you to act, e.g. to give money, volunteer, or join the cause in a more active way. But now, more and more, these organisations find themselves competing in a marketplace where we, their 'customers', are suffering from compassion fatigue. Let's be honest. There are so many worthwhile charities vying for our attention. We are continually asked to make one lowly, humble contribution. We find ourselves wearily asking: can my gift really make a difference?

I am often asked to help charities find a new way to tell their story so that they can better reach their goals. I tell them that's the wrong approach already. The number one question their (and your) audience is asking is, 'Why should I care?' The central desire of anyone listening to a story is that they want to be moved. An audience is always asking: please move me so that I will care. I want to be moved. Please tell me a story that ennobles me.

There are two approaches you can take when it comes to trying to get someone to take action. Present the cold hard facts. Or make an emotional connection. One tends to work, the other less so. You can either pander to someone's guilt, for which they will never forgive you, or you can dare to unlatch their heart, for which they will always be grateful.

Consider these facts about one of our most precious commodities – water:

— 663 million people on this planet do not have safe access to clean water. That's 1 in 10 people worldwide.
— 4,100 children each day die from a lack of safe water.
— Unsafe water kills more people than all forms of violence and war.

In rural Uganda, as in many remote African villages, the person who fetches the water is usually a woman, who can walk at least three miles a day carrying up to ten gallons in two plastic containers. She must then decide how she will use that water during the day: cooking, washing the children or laundering the clothes. Maybe there will be some left over to water the small garden. Mostly, this water is dirty and unsafe. Who can argue with these facts? Who isn't going to feel anger? But will these facts cause you to actually do anything about it?

When we tell a story like this we can either state cold, hard truths, or we can create an emotional connection. One way to do this is to make the story personal. To 'hand over the spark', and tell your audience why *you* care so much about this. What was the singular event that was the catalyst that catapulted you to care enough to get involved? Observe how this is done in the following story.

For years, Scott Harrison led the ultimate wild, hipster, nightclub promoter's lifestyle in the New York club and fashion scene. He had his own mid-town loft by his mid-twenties. His Rolodex featured the unlisted names and numbers of New York's hottest rock, fashion and nightclub elite. It was nothing for his clients, as he put it, 'to blow $365 on a bottle of Grey Goose vodka, before the tip'. He recalls, 'Your life only had meaning if you got past the velvet rope, and then you got wasted or laid'. By his own admission, he was successful, arrogant, and desperately unhappy. And, yeah, 'spiritually bankrupt', having long abandoned his childhood Christian faith.

One night, Scott hit a wall. The constant angling, keeping up with the scene, dealing with all manner of people who were all themselves 'burning the candle at both ends' left Scott exhausted. He decided to take a break, and wanted to re-explore faith and service. He thought, why not spend a year volunteering in some noble, far-off African mission? This seemed like some kind of cool, alternative vacation. He was willing to volunteer, and applied to several humanitarian organisations before quickly learning that no mission would have him. First of all, he had no qualifications. Secondly, they could probably see right through him. However, Scott persisted. He realised he had to offer something. Finally, after some time looking, he found a place. In fact, it was the only place that would take him as a volunteer – purely because he told them he was a photographer. And he was, sort of. He took pictures of models, especially during New York's notorious Fashion Week, and pretty buildings in Europe. Again, he thought he would take off for just a year. He had no idea what was next, but the one thing he knew for sure was that he'd had it with nightlife.

With just this one opening, he took off for the floating hospital, 'Mercy Ship', a humanitarian organisation that offers free medical care to some of the world's poorest nations. Scott had never heard of them before. They don't advertise in New York City. But they provide a place for first-world doctors to donate their vacation time to healing the 'lowest of the low' as the Mercy Ship sails from harbour to harbour around Africa. When Scott entered his cabin, with three single bunks, he was devastated. He'd gone from living like a prince in Manhattan, to living like a pauper. He struggled to do the job. He found himself continually bowled over and in tears. He couldn't bear to take photos of some of the most wretched deformities and tumours humans can suffer. Then one volunteer doctor – who had left his thriving career for a two-week vacation on board the ship, and then stayed on – casually mentioned to Scott that so much of the sickness around the world was simply due to drinking unsafe water.

Scott paused. He took a cold, hard look at his shared cabin, and realised he had so much to be grateful for – not least his good health that he so took for granted. He got off the ship in Liberia and spent time in remote villages, and even in a leper colony because, he said, he simply wanted to 'put a face on the 1.2 billion living in poverty'.

When he returned to New York, Scott studied the $16 cocktails his friends were sending him down the bar to celebrate his homecoming. He decided there and then to put his considerable nightclub promoter's skills – and his enviable Rolodex – into creating an event like no other: The Water Ball. He made it fun, elegant and pure. He told guests that 100 per cent of their money would do this one good, pure thing. With the proceeds he would set up a charity that would fund clear water projects around the world, sometimes drilling deep for water in the most inaccessible regions. Here the pure water was so far underground that no water had been able to be pumped, much less accessed by local drills. He masterfully marketed 'charity: water' using pictures of smiling children playing in the water, and happy village women pumping water from local wells.

With the first drill Scott's charity was able to buy, six freshwater wells were dug in northern Uganda. When the programme director, Becky Shaw, arrived to inspect one of the wells, she said, 'A woman jumped toward me and screamed two inches from my face. I didn't realise that she was actually singing. The high-pitched shrieking was so loud and reverberated with such energy and emotion.'

The woman was Helen Apio, one of many who would wake up every day before dawn, take two five-gallon jerrycans and walk three miles to bring back water for her family. She would have to stand in long lines and often, by the time she reached the front of the queue, the day's water had gone. She would then be forced to bring home contaminated water from the pond. On the way back, she would agonise about how to use it: 'Should I water my garden so we can grow food? Should I use it to cook a meal? Should we drink it? Should I use it to wash the children's school uniforms?' On occasion, her children had been sent home from school because their uniforms were not clean.

Now, standing next to the new well, Helen said to Becky, 'I am happy now. I have time to eat, my children can go to school. And I can even work in my garden, take a shower and then come back for more water if I want! I am bathing so well.'

Becky noted Helen's fresh flowers in her hair, the lovely green dress she was wearing for this special occasion. She touched her arm and said, 'You look great.'

'Yes,' said Helen. Then she paused and said, 'Now, I feel beautiful.'

Since 2006, charity: water's clean water projects have enabled over 7 million people to now get on with their lives. Scott has raised over $260 million for water projects and operations. With this, he's funded over 24,000 clean water projects in 24 countries in some of the remotest, most difficult to access by drill regions of the world. What Scott doesn't now know about drills and geology isn't worth discussing. The charity: water's website, www.charitywater.org, resounds hip, fun, cheerful. You feel drawn in by Scott's ebullience and quality management. His attention to detail. He cares about the 'little things', just like a successful nightclub impresario. He has built his brand by creating a sense of trustworthiness, competence and likeability. And he has done this, in part, by sharing his own story. Undiluted. The moment that led to his personal transformation.

When Scott tells the story behind charity: water, he shares the experience that originally captivated him. He simply hands this to the audience – raw emotion and all – who are moved to help and support the cause. They are moved to act.

On another level, his personal story reveals a more vulnerable side to this once brash nightclub entrepreneur. And we'll hear more about this in the next chapter.

'Only connect.'

—

E.M. Forster

5
Dare to be Vulnerable

First of all, this is no time for therapy. Hindus conjecture that we are layered in samskaras – shrink-wrapped sheaths, like onion-layers – of emotional pain or bad karma. If we are to become fully conscious, mature adults, our job is to break through those layers. Telling our story can help us achieve this but we must be willing to be vulnerable. To show some skin.

A few years ago, I found myself in Wales at the Do Lectures listening to what I thought was a local-interest story – one more relevant to those in the room who lived nearby and stood to benefit from the information.

Shan Williams, a blonde, middle-aged wife and mother, stood up to speak. First, she declared that she had a fear of public speaking. Then she introduced herself – 'For my sins, I am a town councillor' – and said that she was going to share her story of trying to save the dying town of Cardigan in Wales. Cardigan, with a population of 4,000, was once a vibrant brick-making town and a place where the first workmen's clothes were made en masse for the miners. Today, all that is gone. Instead, the young people can't wait to get out of town to make a life elsewhere. The dam on the Mwldan river lies idle, no longer used to generate electricity.

The brickworks is closed. Warehouse-style stores clutter the landscape, along with major supermarket chains which take millions of pounds a week out of the town.

I must confess, at first I listened with polite ... well, fatigue. I thought to myself, This is the story of mature democracies all over the world: the Rust Bowl in Detroit, the abandoned textile mill industry in New England. Even my grandmother's small Kentucky town in the South. When I was a child, I could walk alone to the town centre, visit the local stores and say, 'Hey,' and they all knew me by name. Today, major supermarket chains have wiped out thousands of these towns by building superstores by the highway. My grandmother's town square is now deathly quiet. There's no place for the teenagers to socialise. The once vibrant local factories sold out to China. Now, the superstores sell these Chinese-made products to the local American folks, who suffer from rampant unemployment and live on welfare. I thought to myself, these market forces are so much bigger than us. How can one person possibly make a difference?

Shan continued her story. Apparently, a large parcel of land in Cardigan's town centre had been earmarked for purchase by yet another major supermarket chain. But a petition was circulated and thousands of local citizens signed it. They agreed that this wasn't what their town needed. Shan decided that she would lead the movement, called 4CG which stands for – in Welsh – Cymdeithas Cynal a Chefnogi Cefn Gwlad (in English, 'A Society to Support the Unsustainable Rural Countryside'), to buy that land and build something that the community really did need. More than 650 people supported her. Shares were created, a community movement was born. But they needed a mortgage to purchase the land and there was a deadline: 31 December. The banks were slow to co-operate. It was looking as if the 4CG movement would lose the whole project. On 23 December, Shan, who had been calling the bank manager to no avail, emailed him again only to receive an 'out of office' courtesy email telling her that he was away on annual leave, until 7 January.

Before us, in front of the 100-strong crowd, Shan's lips began to quiver. Her voice full of emotion, she remembered the pain of this moment. 'I was going to have to face all these shareholders and tell them it was over.'

Shan's vulnerability and sheer courage to face this memory woke me up. With just one day left before the Christmas holiday began, Shan went to the Land Registry office to research who owned the underlying land. It was the Allied Irish Bank. Starting at the southern end of the UK, she called every Allied Irish bank manager to ask for help. Not one manager would take her call. Until she reached Liverpool. Shan fought back tears as she recounted each moment that followed, now vivid in her mind's eye. A kind voice came on the line: 'Hello, Shan, this is Mark Dolan. I've been following 4CG. How can I help you?' Shan said quietly, 'We got the loan that day.'

Now, Cardigan has a car park built on the land 4CG bought. Whereas before parking cost one pound, their car park charges a fraction of that and more people are encouraged to come into town and shop locally. With the £1,000 profits it now makes weekly, 4CG have built a day-care centre, museum and eco-shop, as well as a local organic produce market. More recently, Shan and 4CG have created an 'online shopping site to buy local produce' to compete with the big supermarket chains. Shan says, 'If you can't beat them, join them.' Their next project is investigating micro-hydro energy on the Mwldan river.

Then Shan's full vigour came out: 'Why should £4 million a week go out of this town to buy food brought in from other towns and countries? Why should we buy water at £11,000 a week? People in the community once fed themselves with good local food. We once drank our own clean water. From our mills, we made bricks exported the world over. Our bricks built the entire Dublin Harbour. Why should our jobs go away?'

She was about to continue. But, now in rare form, her mouth set in determination, she paused, and then said, 'That's enough for now.' I found myself so wanting more. Out of the two dozen talks I heard that weekend, her story is the one I still ruminate on. What if there had been a Shan Williams – like Atticus Finch in *To Kill A Mockingbird* or George Bailey, aka Jimmy Stewart, in *It's A Wonderful Life* – in my grandmother's small town? What if someone had led the charge?

This is what makes a great story: one person against the system. Courage revealed under intense odds, terrible pressure. Determination winning out. And, in winning the ordinary thing – an area of land to create a car park – the extraordinary character is forged. Shan remains humble, vulnerable, and a standard bearer of warrior energy for all of us.

Shan's determination reminded me of something Muhammad Ali said once: 'Champions have to have last-minute stamina. They have to have the skill and the will. But the will must be stronger than the skill.'

Let's look at the classic elegance of this story and what Shan does perfectly. It resonates. You ruminate on it long afterwards because it came from the truth, and at its heart was Shan's vulnerability. Her fear of failure, of letting down so many well-meaning people who had given her their support. Thinking back to our ten principles of storytelling (p. 22–23), Shan dared to share the emotion. She kept the story interesting, building to its natural endpoint – securing the plot of land. And this was her personal story. What she went through to get to that endpoint. She told the story as if she were telling a friend and, in doing so, she created an emotional connection with the audience present.

Notice how she structured the story. She gave the GPS, a small town in Wales, and context. She explained the 'problem' with facts and actions: the petition to halt the building of yet another superstore; her need to get the bank to act.

It built towards the story's climax. Then when it came to the eleventh hour, her eyes brimmed over with tears, her voice quivered. She had to hold herself back from breaking down. Her passion and vulnerability – how much this meant to her not to disappoint her town – rang through, like a tolling bell. We were compelled by her belief in her story, her emotional intensity. We couldn't help but pay attention.

Once Shan realised that all was basically lost, she took action and did not let go. She called every branch of the bank. (Remember this was 23 December, virtually Christmas Eve. Imagine Shan calling Scrooge and what his response would have been.) Shan's vision required relentless courage and belief. All great stories possess this moment of conscious choice and deliberation. At this point, her actual storytelling slowed down. She had been angry, frustrated, stalled at every turn.

Then, she reported, 'a kind voice came on the line'. Notice the opposite emotion in her memory: kindness. An ease surfaced in Shan's demeanour. A sigh of relief, of letting go. She needed the mortgage to appear and now it was in her grasp. A mortgage is such an ordinary thing in our modern world, but here it became extraordinary.

The pay-off was Shan's restored vigour, even anger and determination. And then she left the stage. Obviously, she had more to impart. She left us desperate to know more. And, she ennobled us in her parting.

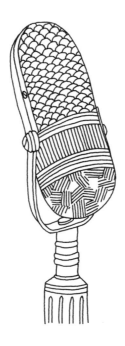

'Forget about the microphone,
just speak to me. As a friend.'

—

Lionel Logue to King George VI, *The King's Speech*

6
The Story Behind The Story

We can never get enough of the stories that we love.
Consider the film adaptations of bestselling books
such as Harry Potter or *The Hunger Games*. Even
though audiences already know these stories, and
more to the point, their ending, they still clamour for
the immersive, sight and sound, cinematic experience.
There's something hugely enjoyable about sharing
familiar stories with loved ones, while gathered
before the big screen, as if we were sitting around a
flickering campfire. But how do you make a story
fresh and interesting?

With cinematic storytelling, bitter box-office experience
has proven that the 'known' story must find a new
angle for the film version to attract an audience, even
with core fans. This new angle must possess audacity.
A fresh perspective that dares to show the character in
a vulnerable, if not embarrassing, light, at some point
in their life journey. So often this is the real story, or the
'story behind the story'. The hidden narrative that holds it
all together. In many cases this will compel an even larger
audience to identify with a character – even if it's one
where the broad facts are already known.

For example, *The Social Network* (Columbia, 2010), written by Aaron Sorkin, is the story of Mark Zuckerberg, the Harvard student who created Facebook in 2003, just seven years before the film's release. This multiple award-winning film took this world-famous phenomenon and told us the story behind the story. The number one question Sorkin had to address was: even if we love Facebook, why should we care about its inventor? For the movie to succeed, Sorkin had to find a vulnerability about the central character that would compel us to engage with the story. It also had to be a universal truth – one we could relate to in our own lives.

In this case, *The Social Network* is essentially about the 'loneliest man on earth'. A 20-something billionaire with 500 million 'friends' who betrays everyone who ever cared for him, and in the end can't even get his former girlfriend to accept his 'friend' request. *The Social Network* is the universal retelling of the 'big idea' concept: What is it to gain the whole world and lose your soul?

So it was with the recent retelling of the story of the British King, George VI. During World War Two, David Seidler (screenwriter of *The King's Speech*) was a little boy who suffered from a terrible stammer. Having been brought to New York to escape London's blitz, David listened to the king's every speech on the radio, and innately understood what George VI had had to endure simply to be able to inspire his people during this difficult time. King George VI became his hero. Eventually becoming a screenwriter, and with this story always close to his heart, he wrote to the Queen Mother to ask her permission to tell the story of her late husband. Immediately, an envelope from Buckingham Palace arrived with an impressive red seal on the envelope. The Queen Mother's private secretary wrote back to say that she would not give her permission. But at the bottom of the typewritten missive, the Queen Mother wrote, in her own handwriting, 'Please, not in my lifetime.' It was too painful. David, being an obedient British subject, put aside the project. He did not think she would live to be 101.

Years later, after the Queen Mother passed away, David revisited the script. He now had more than 30 years' experience as a screenwriter and, finally, he embarked on his project to tell the real story of George VI: a stammering king in the age of the radio. The stammer was all the more embarrassing, because the then Duke of York (who would become King George VI in 1936) was forced to speak 'live' to the entire British Empire during the age when the radio had become ubiquitous. If the Duke of York had been born a generation earlier, he could have just waved from a horse. A generation later, he could have been edited.

To simply retell the various episodes of George's life would be, well, boring. And, if that is all the story had been, Seidler's script would still be in his drawer. In fact, even with this new audacious angle, when Seidler first posited the idea for *The King's Speech*, no one saw its potential. For sure, no Hollywood studio wanted to finance this film as they felt it was too small a story. They felt it would only be of interest to a niche audience of older Brits who remembered that era.

What David had to find was the story behind the story, its Big Idea, or theme. Why should any of us care about a rich man, a royal who had an extraordinarily privileged life? In short, to appreciate the life of this extraordinary man, we needed to experience him as an ordinary man with fears that are universal.

We know from the beginning what 'Bertie', as the king was known, wants. He wants to be able to speak fluently and eloquently when giving a public address. But, as it turns out, he needs to get in touch with his worst fear:

his fear of becoming king. Would he have what it takes to be king? How will he break through this physical manifestation of his fear? The story that David Seidler tells is that it was through the unlikely friendship with a commoner, Lionel Logue – an Australian – who is perhaps the only person in the Empire who believed Bertie would make a 'bloody great king' and gives him the confidence that helps him to overcome his stammer.

As king, he will have to both serve his people and speak in public, and give live broadcasts on the radio, throughout World War Two. David Seidler's brilliant storytelling gives us not one but two stories: that of an extraordinary man, Bertie (soon to become George VI), who becomes ordinary before our eyes, and secondarily, that of an ordinary man, Lionel Logue, who becomes extraordinary for his friendship and belief in George VI. It is Lionel Logue and this great unsung friendship that, in this case, creates the story behind the story.

For the real story here is that Bertie had never known a commoner. He'd never even had a friend, beyond his beloved wife. Through facing his fear of public speaking, he makes the first true friend of his life. And it is only by getting to know the common man, Lionel, that he is able to lead and serve his people through a terrible war. Their friendship opens his humanity, and allows him to become revered as a beloved king. Indeed, because the British had known him as an embarrassing public speaker, and then witnessed his resilience to overcome this affliction, they could relate to his courage that shone through ever more powerfully when he spoke to the entire Empire over the BBC, on the night of 3 September 1939, when Great Britain declared war on Germany. Thus, he went on to become a great symbol of resilience to the British.

This little story that no Hollywood studio would finance,

because it was really 'two men in a room talking; and one of them was stuttering', was made for $15 million, taking their producers several years to raise the money. Within three months of release, it had made over $415 million, won the Academy Award for Best Film, Director, Screenplay and Actor, and seven BAFTAs.

This film would not have happened had it not been for David Seidler's personal connection to the king in suffering from the same affliction.

The story behind the story is always personal. Consider George Lucas and his love of hot rods, fully embracing the California teen car culture in the late 1950s and early 60s. On 12 June 1962, George found himself pulled out of his souped-up Autobianchi Biachina when another driver broadsided him and his car twisted itself around a tree. He should have died. From this near-death experience George vowed that he would pursue his dreams. He went on to place his love of hot rods, vehicles and hardware into his film *American Graffiti*, and then the intergalactic epic masterpiece, the *Star Wars* franchise.

It could be argued that President Barack Obama would not have been elected if he had not written his own memoirs, *Dreams from My Father: A Story of Race and Inheritance*, wherein he dares to share his journey growing up as a mixed-race child in America – the land still at odds with its racist legacy. His election was an absolute sea change in the United States, but it could not have happened had Americans not felt comfortable with Obama's personal story. He gave them his back story before he was famous – before any journalists or tabloids could attempt to create a story for him. This was very smart, and a great example for what all of us must do today, if we want to succeed.

So if you want to secure that job, for example, global headhunter Bill Simon says that during the interview process it is 'emotional resonance' that those conducting the interview will remember. 'When you tell a purposeful story demonstrating your attitude and passion, suddenly the data, facts and figures of your CV become memorable. The story you tell will hit your listeners' hearts and stay top of mind long after you've left.'

Tuning into the truth of our own story can be daunting for any of us. Our first impulse is to deflect our stories, by saying that they're all too common, that no one would be interested. Why should anyone (but your mother) care? But, in fact, tuning into your own story is your power. We are all unique. We have all faced difficult circumstances, experienced triumphs, setbacks and disappointments. But it is how we have made our choices in the face of adversity – how we harnessed courage at our own thresholds – that makes each of us unique and exceptional. This is the story others want to hear. This is why you need to tell your story. And tell it well.

And, now, you are so close to becoming an expert storyteller, you can probably almost *feel* it. So next, let's find out why and how our sense memories can truly elevate a story.

'We do not need magic to change
the world, we carry all the power
we need inside ourselves already:
we have the power to imagine better.'

—

J.K. Rowling

'The act of simply lifting out any of the senses –
whether it's the sense of sight, touch, hearing,
smell or taste. Isolating one of them alone
always creates an emotional connection.'

—

David Lynch

7
Evoke the Senses

So often, evoking a sense memory can create a strong
and lasting bond with the listener. A sensory retelling
of a story will help your audience to 'feel' it and, if the
sense is particularly evocative, allow it to linger long
after the telling has ended. Of the five senses, one
is always more dominant during a particular event
or experience. The next story draws on one sense
in particular: taste. By evoking it and using it in her
narrative, one woman was able to change the way that
millions of us bought and consumed our food.

Alice Waters is an American chef and food activist.
She is the owner of the internationally renowned Chez
Panisse restaurant in Berkeley, California, famous for
its locally grown ingredients, oak-fired pizza ovens,
and for pioneering the California Cuisine organic food
movement. She is also co-founder of the slow food and
farmers' market movements, and the Edible Schoolyard
programme. Alice is even credited as the inspiration for
the salad as we now know it in America. You can trace
the common household staple, the pre-washed lettuce
mélange available at supermarkets everywhere, back to
her. I know this because I always think of Alice in grateful

awe when I shop for salad. Throughout my childhood growing up in America's south, if your meal came with a salad that meant a slab of green jello, quivering upon a lifeless leaf of iceberg lettuce. Atop the jello was a shot of mayonnaise with a bright red maraschino cherry in the centre. Healthy? I don't think so. Alice Waters spear-headed a revolution that transformed how and where we shop for food; our plates, and our palates. She didn't do it out of a sense of mission. She did it because what she sought was simply 'taste'. She wanted to bring back the true pleasure of eating to create a sense of well-being. So how did she use sense memory to bring about this change?

To begin at the beginning, Alice happened to be a student at the University of California, Berkeley, on 2 December 1964 when political activist Mario Savio famously urged the students to 'put your bodies upon the gears'. This passionate speech begat the Berkeley Free Speech Movement, which set off the counter-culture movement, which also instigated massive non-violent (mostly) protests against the Vietnam War. Everything was thrown up in the air, especially in Berkeley.

In the midst of all this, Alice, who was a French literature major, took a semester off to study in France. What Alice encountered in Paris – then, as now – were city markets replenished with locally grown, fresh produce. This was, and is, a daily affair. Alice came home to California with a new-found love of food, made from fresh, non-homogenised, local produce. She'd also learned to cook and loved nothing more than cooking for her friends during these rich, debate-heavy Berkeley days. She wanted to create a home-like restaurant and in 1971 she opened 'Chez Panisse', in homage to French novelist Marcel Pagnol.

But where was she going to find fresh food here in

America such as she'd found in Paris? This is where I don't know whether to find this part of the American story ironic or tragic. As every child learns in elementary school, the great American tomato is actually a fruit. Tomatoes were staple produce grown in everyone's backyards. Come August, kitchens would be overflowing with ripe, rich, juicy bright red tomatoes. But, starting in the 1960s, when major supermarkets began to supplant the local grocery stores, there soon appeared – ubiquitously and bountiful – large, flavourless tomatoes from mega-farms; the same farms that drove so many of the local farmers out of business. Soon, the backyard gardens seemed to be a thing of the past. Supermarket tomatoes were now super big, but they had been cultivated so they could be shipped long distances. To this day, I cannot eat a store-bought tomato. Once you cut into its rubbery orange-red skin, the inner fruit is white. They taste bland, like eating Styrofoam.

One day I found my mother's high-school annual from the 1940s. All the girls appeared slender and toned. I compared it to my own from the early seventies in which all my friends looked, well, overweight. Later that day I needed to go on the weekly grocery run. I walked through the brightly lit, air-conditioned, muzak'd food aisles of our supermarket. For miles, it seemed, one could only see bruised apples, limp lettuces, white bread, frozen ready meals, cookies labelled with cute names like 'Debbie' and 'Little Susies'. There were vast towering displays of sugar-coated breakfast cereals. I parked my creaky shopping cart and walked out. I asked myself, 'When did we adapt to this life of one-stop-shopping and eating food devoid of any health value whatsoever?'

Meanwhile, Alice Waters was researching California's rich heartland valley – the geographical equivalent to the verdant Tigris–Euphrates valley – and discovered a number of small farming communities producing their own food.

In pursuit of ripe, organic strawberries, Alice flew from San Francisco to San Diego – a 500-mile journey. On the return flight, a New York food magazine editor, who was travelling with her, watched, mouth agape, as Alice carried a large basket of strawberries on to the plane and held it on her lap. The smell overwhelmed everyone on the flight. Hands reached into the basket with requests to taste 'just one'. Alice obliged, even though she knew that it would probably mean arriving home with an empty basket. She looked at the food editor, eyes aglow, saying, 'I think we're on to something here.'

When I discovered Chez Panisse – Alice Waters' oasis of taste and beauty in hip Berkeley, I couldn't believe how, well, soothing it was. She had installed her restaurant in a 1920s Arts and Crafts-style bungalow. Copper-topped candle carriers created natural, ambient lighting. A wonderful oak-fired fresh pizza oven greeted you in the dining room – a revolutionary presence at that time. Alice had managed to persuade the oven-maker in a small pizza restaurant near Turin to build her one specifically for the restaurant. Every night, just as the restaurant opened, a waiter would set a rosemary twig alight so that the fragrance filled the room. And, the butter! So fresh! I couldn't understand why this place should be so extraordinary, but it simply was.

I followed reports of Alice's career, as one might cut out the clippings of a favourite movie star. I loved reading about Alice sharing the organic strawberries on the airplane with all the captivated passengers; or hearing that at a major conference presided over by none other than Julia Child, the doyenne of French cooking, Alice appealed for locally grown, organic produce. Child was taken aback and remonstrated with Alice, saying, 'My dear, I think you underestimate the quality available from our own supermarkets.' But here it was: two generations colliding. And Alice envisioned something different. Something better. Something available to everyone. She was on a mission. She was, indeed, putting her 'body on the gears'.

Alice decreed that she needed to source locally grown organic food daily. The menu in Chez Panisse would change according to what was available on the day. Others thought she was being too precious. Why not do what was always done, order food in bulk, and stock it in a large refrigerator. Instead, Alice created a campaign wherein she enticed local farmers, orchard growers, livestock ranchers and fisheries to supply her restaurant. Her 'quiet revolution' soon grew in reputation both in the US and around the world. Her demand raised up a network of expert organic farmers. The California Farmers' Market movement was born and goes from strength to strength.

As I witnessed Alice's restaurant grow in stature – winning international culinary awards – I thought back to what I had found confounding, and even distasteful. I had become discouraged that 'major market forces' had taken over our daily bread. But Alice, on the other hand, had simply followed her passion. She let her love of taste, and her passionate pursuit of the best that this sense could offer, create a market for daily goodness. Literally the bread of life. She was mastering the art of well-being.

What a good idea she had. We now often talk about a tweet or YouTube video going viral. But the compounding value of a great idea, handed around person to person, is what has always moved civilisation forward. From time immemorial. Incrementally, Alice's food revolution finally reached the White House.

For years, Alice campaigned to persuade the residents

of the White House to build an organic garden. Former presidents' wives sent letters complimenting Alice on the success of her famous restaurant. The Clintons dined there whenever they were in town, Hillary going so far as to write Alice a nice note that she and Bill had herb pots on their balcony. Yet Alice was not satisfied that the country's political leaders understood the gravity of the 'taste' and health issues at stake here. She appealed to the media, saying, 'Good food should be a right and not a privilege. It should be grown without pesticides and herbicides. Everybody deserves this food.'

When Alice's only child, Fanny, entered Berkeley's Martin Luther King Middle School, Alice was scandalised to see how poor the school diet was. The students would buy their lunches out of junk-food vending machines. Alice asked the school for the use of a broken-asphalt playground area. She raised the money and had an organic garden planted, with the students taking part at each stage – from seeding to daily cultivation to harvest. She even had an outdoor pizza oven built surrounded by edible flowers. When the top-rated US television show *60 Minutes* shot the story, the reporter was surprised to observe how engaged the students were with their hands-on encounter with growing. They made dough and baked pizza in the outdoor oven. On camera, this group of giggling, chatting 12-year-old students all fell into a kind of reverie. Quietly, they pulled out their fresh-baked pizzas and ate them. They were the visible embodiment of well-being.

Alice had nearly given up on the White House, until the Obamas came in. She wrote to them, asking them to set an example for America: of caring for the environment, healthy eating, and growing your own. But Michelle Obama was already on to this. Michelle's first project was to create an organic vegetable garden, along with beehives, on the

White House lawn. Her mission was the 'Let's Move!' campaign to raise awareness of the childhood obesity epidemic in America. The *New York Times* reported that childhood obesity numbers declined 5 per cent in several key states for the first time in 30 years.

An article in the *San Francisco Chronicle* stated: 'Obama's Let's Move! campaign ... addresses much of what Waters has been preaching ... Chris Lehane, a political consultant who has worked for Al Gore and Bill Clinton, sees Waters as "the George Washington of the movement and Northern California as the 13 colonies ... If you're going to pick a figure who's responsible for it, it all comes back to her".'

Alice's story reveals a surprise. We discover something we had almost forgotten, and didn't even know we'd lost. At heart, her story is a journey of restoration, taking us back to the source of our well-being through the sense memory: taste. Alice also had vision. She believed that a vital network could be built sustainably – of organic farmers, orchards, ranchers and fisheries – so that we could, indeed, have quality food. She passionately believed that by nurturing culinary talent and creating a market for those restaurants that would prepare locally grown fresh food, the simple pleasure of eating tasty, wholesome food would be elevated. Alice's vision resulted in a surprising gift: the restoration of community, an interconnected world. There was 'healing in the land', if you like. This is a classic story of transformation within a generation, passed on to the next. The world was changed.

Sadly, Alice received a blow in 2013 when Chez Panisse suffered a terrible fire that caused widespread damage. Fittingly, Alice issued this eloquent response the very next morning:

'Exactly 31 years ago today, we had our first fire at the

restaurant that destroyed the wall separating the dining room from the kitchen. We never rebuilt that wall and it changed Chez Panisse completely, establishing that beautiful connection between the kitchen and the dining room. It is vitally important that things are renewed and restored and we have already begun the process of rebuilding.'

Alice has become a heroine of mine. Certainly, we have shared the same times, and I have admired her choices. Her story is one that so beautifully evokes the senses. Yours may not be quite so pronounced but highlighting one of the key senses produces not only a more visceral story but one that will linger with the listener for far longer. As David Lynch so aptly put it – and as many great storytellers ably employ – the simple act of isolating one sense somehow does provide the most direct emotional connection to your audience.

'Be the change you wish to see in the world.'

—

Gandhi

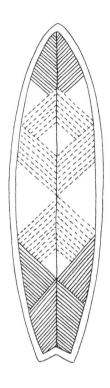

'Real adventure is defined best
as a journey from which you may
not come back alive, and certainly
not as the same person.'

—

Yvon Chouinard

8
The Journey is the Story

In March 2017, *Forbes* listed Yvon Chouinard, owner of Patagonia, as one of 12 Notable New Billionaires. A spokeswoman for Patagonia immediately shot back this reply to *Forbes*, 'We strongly oppose being included on this list.' According to today's standards, wouldn't most people be thrilled to be declared a billionaire and want to be in this esteemed group?

But Chouinard, a former 1960s-era dropout, explained, 'I've been a businessman for almost 60 years. It's as difficult for me to say those words as it is for someone to admit being an alcoholic.' Chouinard shares his journey towards becoming a world-class businessman in his bestseller, *Let My People Go Surfing: The Education of a Reluctant Businessman* – a rare combination of a first-rate business treatise extolled by *Harvard Business Review* and a Boy's Own adventure.

Born in 1938, the son of French-Canadian immigrants, Yvon grew up in suburban Burbank, California, where he discovered a passion for falconry and rock-climbing – the latter he attempted in slippery tennis shoes. In his book, Yvon reveals how, as a teenager, he decided to become the first man to climb the North American wall on El Capitan in Yosemite – one of the sheerest, most dramatically beautiful and emblematic rock faces in the world. Yvon fell into his business *because* he needed to create specific gear for his rock-climbing passion. So he learned blacksmithing in order to forge the kind of iron pitons he had devised for this high-risk sport. He sold them out of the trunk of his car and named his company Chouinard Equipment, Ltd. His single-page mimeographed sales sheet at the time stated, 'Delivery unreliable between April and October.' In other words, Yvon's surfing and rock climbing season.

Chouinard said, 'We took special pride in the fact that climbing rock and icefalls had no economic value in society. Politicians and businessmen ... and corporations were the source of all evil.' But this is not the story of this chapter. A journey in storytelling vernacular – from Homer's *Odyssey* to *Lawrence of Arabia* (or any great film) – is quite simply a journey within your own character and soul.

From all my years of story analysis and as we touched on in chapter 6, I've learned that if anyone undergoes a 180-degree transformation – such as Yvon, from defiant hippy to world-class businessman – there is always a deeper truth to uncover, because his story is the journey to transformation. Yvon's 'true life journey' involves friendship, in particular, his close bond with another 60s-era dropout, Doug Tompkins, a kind of soulmate brother. This is the story of the lifelong journey they undertook together – to recapture the wild within themselves, to revisit the wild in their personal adventures amidst their careers building global businesses, and in their separate missions to preserve the wild for future generations.

Their story really begins in 1968, when one drunken night in San Francisco they hatched a plan to take off for six months. It would be a trip of a lifetime to explore untouched mountain ranges and un-surfed coastline on an 8,000-mile expedition from California to deepest Patagonia. Tompkins' wife, Susie, had given birth just two weeks before. Nevertheless, the two men and a couple of other friends packed an old Ford van with surfboards, skis and gear, and drove south from California to Argentina. They called themselves the Fun Hogs.

One hot, humid day, they stopped to cool off in a jungle river in Colombia. Wiping his brow with his red bandana, Yvon suddenly decided to dive head-first off the bridge into the water below. Doug laughed at his best mate's typical audacious verve. Then paused. Yvon was not coming up for air. 'Holy shit!' – Yvon was floating, upside-down, unconscious.

Doug ran down the ravine, jumped in and pulled out his friend. Yvon had suffered a compression fracture of the neck. Fortunately, not so badly that they couldn't continue their journey. Their holy grail was Mount Fitz Roy, an 11,000-foot rock tower in Argentina. A mountain that had been climbed only twice before.

As they began their climb, an ice storm blew in leaving them stranded on the side of the mountain. They refused to give up. 'We spent 31 days in a snow cave. That was grim,' Chouinard recalled. As soon as the weather cleared, they climbed up to the summit. They stayed for about 20 minutes before deciding it was time to head home. Because as Yvon said, 'How we climbed the mountain was more important than reaching the top.'

Neither man was the same after that trip. They returned to their families in Northern California. In 1964, Doug and his wife Susie started the successful outdoor clothing brand North Face – so called because the north face is the coldest part of any mountain, and he would know. They sold that company (which went on to become a major brand).

They then started selling on-trend girls' dresses at street markets. In a matter of years, they had built Susie's new brand into an international, multi million-dollar teen clothing company, Esprit.

Meanwhile, Yvon, who still wanted to source better outdoor clothing, began importing rugby shirts from the UK. His newly named company, Patagonia, took the silhouette of Fitz Roy as its logo.

Yvon maintained his practice of leading by MBA (Management By Absence). He introduced the corporate lifestyle practice of giving his employees and himself flexi-time. As long as they got their work done, they could take time off to surf, ski, climb and work on environmental causes. The company grew steadily, if modestly, until 1980 when Yvon's wife, Malinda, discovered synchilla – a fabric made from recycled soda-pop bottles, available in wild colours such as fuchsia, neon blue and cherry red. Overnight, it seemed, Patagonia became a fashion sensation. Profits soared to $100 million. Yvon was now being called the Gucci of outdoor clothing.

Meanwhile, Doug and Susie's company, Esprit, was facing the demanding quarterly cycle of staying hip, young and fashion-forward worldwide. Now, it would seem, both men were tied to their clothing empires. Their businesses were running them. However, they remained friends and would take off for the occasional ten-day adventure to decompress from their busy lives.

Then, one day in the late 1980s, Yvon sent Doug a note: Would he donate $50,000 to buy a huge swathe of pristine mountain-to-sea land in Chile? The land, once owned by Pinochet's men and primed for development, was going cheap. Buying this land could hopefully support the conservation of their beloved Patagonia. Doug paid immediately. But then chose to do more. He flew down to Patagonia and observed first-hand what a windfall opportunity this was: to buy up and preserve into perpetuity thousands of acres of true wilderness before it was too late. He decided to leave his life in San Francisco. He and Susie divorced. Doug took his half of the company earnings (around $125 million) and began to buy land in Chile and Argentina with the aim of giving it back, once national parks had been created and a viable plan of preservation had been established.

Then, Yvon faced a similar life choice. On 31 July 1991, a series of bad business decisions forced Patagonia to lay off 120 employees – 20% of its workforce – a day Yvon called 'Black Friday – the worst day of my life'. Yvon hated it. He had never wanted to be a businessman. As Patagonia had grown, so did all the attendant lawsuits. Supply chain problems assailed him. It was an opportunity for Yvon to sell the company. And that's what everyone counselled him to do.

But he had his own epiphany: what if he could make business work *for* him? What if he could do it on *his* terms? If what was good for business could also be good for the planet? If he could achieve this, then he would have more money to *do* good. So he reinvented his entire business practice.

Yvon knew that he loved the great outdoors. He loved breaking the rules. Quoting Socrates he said, 'The unexamined life is not worth living.' For months, Yvon went back to basics. He sat down with his employees and brainstormed what Patagonia could be as a successful business. 'And it was very important that we were successful, otherwise, no one would listen,' said Yvon.

Though it was far more expensive, he decided to source organic cotton. He educated his customers with his lavish newsletters featuring beautiful wilderness photographs, facts about conservation and environmental issues – and, of course, his products. He explained why he refused to use 'orange' dye because it was toxic, for example. The more he informed his consumers, the more expensive the costs in his supply chain choices became. Yet his profits escalated by 25% – even in the middle of the 2008–2010 financial crisis. They tripled thereafter. Yvon realised again that, 'Quality is the best business plan. Whenever we do what's right for the planet, we end up making far more money than we could ever have imagined.' Reasoning that the consumer knows what is best for the world and is prepared to pay more for it.

He established 1% for the Planet, an alliance of member businesses each donating a tithe of 1% of pre-tax sales profit to environmental causes. Over the years, Patagonia has given millions of dollars to over 1,000 environmental groups. And over 400 companies have signed up to this initiative.

Yvon continued to donate to Doug's Tompkins Conservation, a diverse range of projects in Chile and Argentina. But Doug was facing extraordinarily tough opposition in Chile. At the time in South America, there was no precedent for private individuals – much less foreigners – spending gargantuan sums to save large areas of wilderness. 'People thought he was a spy at first,' says Claudio Seebach, a former adviser to Chilean president Sebastián Piñera. 'Nobody believed he would really give the land back.' He was publicly derided as *arrogante*, because he dared to tell the Chilean people that their dreams to develop their countryside, rather than preserve it, were wrong. He was attacked from all sides; there were death threats. Yet despite the controversy, Yvon and Doug took off periodically to kayak and hike in the region. On one of these trips, Yvon invited the CEO of Patagonia,

Kristine McDivitt, to join them. Doug and Kristi quickly realised they shared the same vision – to rescue and preserve a true wilderness. Soon they married and became an eco-power couple.

In spite of these battles, in 2010 Yvon and Doug decided to recreate their 1968 expedition from California to the Patagonia mountains. Now in their seventies, both men were planning to make one more historic climb on an unnamed mountain; one that they effectively owned. Both of them had by now bought millions of acres in Patagonia with their wealth, which they put into the Conservacion Patagonica charity. A feature documentary, *180 Degrees South*, followed this journey. In the final scene, the team roasts freshly caught oysters over an open campfire. Yvon sips the fresh oyster juice with relish while he takes in the rising moon. He says, simply, 'This is enough. This is all you need.'

Together, Doug and Kristi carried on, deeply invested in their vision to create a national park system like the US National Parks which had just reintroduced the grey wolf back into Yellowstone. They hoped to see the jaguar, amongst other endangered species, returned to the region. Then, Doug began deeding the land to the public. By 2015, he had created three national parks in Argentina and two in Chile, and he was pushing for the creation of several more.

One of these, Parque Patagonia, is just south of the 90-mile-long General Carrera Lake in southern Chile. In December 2015, the 72-year-old Tompkins and 77-year-old Chouinard, along with climber Rick Ridgeway and three others, went on a five-day, 50-mile kayak paddle to enjoy this volcanic lake and its unique exposed marble caves. Doug had described the trip as 'Just for old times' sake. To keep our hand in, to build a bit of muscle tone.' But, on the fourth day, the group suddenly ran into what Chouinard called a perfect storm. 'We had 40-mile-per-hour winds at our back,' he says. 'Then we got this side wind, so we had huge waves coming in on either side.'

Yvon and his kayak partner were able to paddle to shore. But Doug's kayak capsized. They called for help from a satellite phone. For over an hour, Doug and his kayak partner struggled in frigid volcanic lake water until Doug passed out. He was airlifted to a local hospital. Several hours later, to the world's astonishment, Doug died of hyperthermia.

'We just weren't prepared,' Chouinard admitted later. 'I mean, he was dressed in pressed chinos, a Brooks Brothers shirt, a light sweater and a rain jacket. Like that Zen painter who always leaves part of his painting unfinished, we always left room for disaster.'

Perhaps it is ironic that the man who made his fortune from clothing recounts his close friend's death in terms of what he was wearing. You can feel the rueful humility in his scant comments about how ineffectual these world-class outdoorsmen were at saving their friend's life, in the face of how unforgiving nature can be.

After news of his death spread, Tompkins' grand vision for his holdings got one more boost. 'The presidents of Argentina and Chile called,' said Chouinard, 'and said, 'Hey, let's get the rest of these parks done.''

On 15 March 2017, the world press covered the event: Chilean president Michelle Bachelet signed an agreement with Kristine McDivitt Tompkins, the widow of American conservationist Doug Tompkins. Tompkins Conservation agreed to donate one million acres for new national parks in the largest private donation of its kind for the South American nation. The Tompkins already rank as the greatest private wilderness conservationists of all time, having bought and preserved 2.2 million acres of mountains, rivers and rainforest in Chile and Argentina. An area equivalent to about three Yosemite National Parks.

This may well be why when two months later, in May 2017, the Forbes headline that Yvon Chouinard was a billionaire made him so angry. He said, 'Every individual spends an entire lifetime creating and evolving a personal image that others perceive.' For Yvon, *how* he has climbed the mountain of success has been far more important than reaching the top. Nothing else matters.

Applying the Tools of Storytelling

Dare to be vulnerable
Daring to tell the journey of your story can feel risky.
To reveal the why of your life choices – the embarrassing moments, the emotional, gut-wrenching experiences that define our lives – can seem, well, too vulnerable. But this is the sole reason we tell stories – to connect in truth, and to enable others to 'carry our fire'. The story in this chapter has an ironic ending in that both men dared to tame the wild – a very contradiction in terms. What feelings does it evoke in you?

Juxtaposition
From the first paragraph, two ideas collide. When Forbes extols Yvon Chouinard for becoming a billionaire, he renounces this accolade. Who does this and why, we ask ourselves? The two journeys of becoming world-class businessmen versus pursuing personal adventure seem to be at odds – until they come together towards the chapter's end. Are there similar developments in your own story?

The very spirit of Yvon Chouinard and Doug Tompkins' friendship is an exultation of a life well-lived – the pursuit of their passion to be wild, experience the wild, preserve the wild. Until, inexorably, they face their limits at the mercy of the wild. Again, note how the irony of this truth affects you. Can you name this emotion(s)?

Gleaming Detail – and the use of the Rule of Three

Clothing is the predominant visual motif because it was the basis of both Chouinard and Tompkins' financial wealth. Note that I purposely chose to emphasise – three times – what they were wearing during three risky adventures. Yvon survived the first two events, but the third ended in disaster that might have been survived if Doug had been appropriately dressed for their kayaking trip (but maybe not).

To create the greatest emphasis on the underlying theme of a story, economise on the use of the Gleaming Detail. There is mystery and emotional power in simply reducing this key element to three appearances. The term 'Rule of Three' is universally used in storytelling, music and in life. As the French say, 'Jamais deux sans trois.' ('Never two without three.')

Let go. Hand over your story. Leave the audience wanting more

This chapter ends simply, with just two quotes from Yvon regarding his best friend's untimely death. There is not much available publicly about Yvon's response to this personal tragedy. We are left to surmise his feelings *only by his actions* in his later public business life. This feels true to who Yvon is as a man, and how he wants to be remembered. As Tompkins said about his legacy vision to build twelve national parks in Patagonia, 'Who wants a tomb? Wouldn't you rather have people walking in the wild into perpetuity?'

'Here's to the crazy ones.'

—

Steve Jobs

9
Make the Personal Universal

After almost three decades of storytelling experience, for me few people have demonstrated as great a gift for communication as Steve Jobs. He took the complex realm of computer science and previously 'nerd' inventions and made them cool, even sexy. He possessed the soul of a showman – that unique talent to sell wonder. He intuitively understood that stories are how we all see; they fire up our imaginations. Stories become a conduit to the Big Idea of what our future could be.

Stories are the sole means by which we can envision our own place in the world. Every time Steve had to sell an idea or product, he anchored this abstract idea to a personal moment, event or experience of his own – making himself vulnerable in the process. But his overarching passion was always to 'sell the idea of personal creativity' as a kind of revolution and right that would inexorably improve the universal good.

Even more importantly, he saw this as if it was already happening now. And the only way he knew how to do this was by telling a personal story with a 'long view' – as only a visionary can. Here's a brief look at three of his most illustrative 'storytelling moments' in a vastly

transformative time in the personal computer revolution.
They are also stories revealing the humanity of a man
whose public persona has been much misunderstood.
A man whose life was cut short by his untimely death.
In the words of Edna St. Vincent Millay, 'The candle that
burns twice as bright, burns half as long.'

Steve Jobs, co-founder, chairman and CEO of Apple Inc
was, by all accounts, a visionary. In 1976, at the age of 21,
he co-founded Apple Computer, Inc with Steve Wozniak
(the creator, builder and designer of Apple I). Together
they worked out of the Jobs' family garage in modest,
suburban Los Altos, California. Steve himself could not
code. He never built a computer. He explained then his
sole purpose: 'I just want to make a dent in the universe.'
His life exemplifies the Oxford English Dictionary
definition of a visionary leader: 'A person with original
ideas about what the future will or could be like.'

None of our lives has been the same since he foisted
his vision on the world: that a personal computer could
be like 'a bicycle for the mind', and once we were all wired
and connected *personally*, ideas and productivity would
flourish – and creativity would know no bounds.

One year later, in 1977, Steve became a multimillionaire
at the age of just 22 when the Apple II became one of the
first highly successful mass-produced personal computers.
Three years later, Steve's visit to Xerox PARC in Palo
Alto led him to discover the mouse-driven graphical
user interface (GUI). This was what he was looking for: a
breakthrough in a far more natural, human connective use
of computers. Steve led Apple into a whole new direction,
creating the game-changing Macintosh computer and
ushering in the rise of desktop publishing. The Macintosh
was introduced to the world in 1984 by its now-legendary

Super Bowl advertisement directed by Ridley Scott (still considered the most famous ad ever created). But this first Macintosh was not financially successful, not yet what it promised the world. Steve was difficult. By his own admission, he was an 'arrogant' leader. In 1985, Steve was fired by his own board.

So, Steve went into 'exile' for 11 years. During this time, he married and fathered three children with his wife, Laurene Powell. He already had a daughter, Lisa Brennan-Jobs, by his former partner, Chrisann Brennan. Steve spent his entire $150 million fortune (keeping only one share of Apple stock), developing NeXT, the computer system he believed was the operating system of the future (when no one else did). In addition, he bought a fledgling computer animation company, Pixar, believing in the vision of its founders – Ed Catmull and John Lasseter – that one day they could make a completely computer-generated feature-length animation film. Steve's only mandate: just make it insanely great. Later Steve recalled, 'I couldn't not do what I'd always loved.' He spent his fortune, went into debt, sought investors, sweated out the long gestation of Pixar's first movie, *Toy Story*. Meanwhile, the personal computer world became dominated by Microsoft's monster shares of the market, and Apple Inc became less relevant.

By 1997, Apple Inc was only one quarter away from bankruptcy when the board asked Steve to come back as i-CEO ('i' stood for 'interim'). No one believed Apple could possibly survive. Steve knew he had to give his team, his investors and his eventual customers a vision of why anyone should commit to buy an Apple product – one that hadn't even been designed or built yet. This is when Steve 'bet the ranch'. He spent Apple's remaining advertising budget on a commercial that he wrote with advertising agency, Chiat Day – which became the iconic

'Think different' advert. In just one minute a montage of 20th-century geniuses and visionaries – from Einstein to Richard Branson to Muhammad Ali to Amelia Earhart – stare at us in black and white as the narrator begins, 'Here's to the crazy ones, the misfits, the rebels...' and goes on to extol the virtues of those who dare to 'Think different'. These are the ones who change the world. Inspiring. Haunting. Only at the end do we see the simple Apple logo – the apple with one bite missing. Steve dared his future customers to 'Think different', to align themselves with the very visionaries who, he declared, would no doubt have owned an Apple. He had to plant in everyone's mind's eye a vision of the future, how a personal computer would eventually empower you. He made it personal. In short, you were a genius, too, to even think this way. Soon, Steve became the full chairman and CEO of Apple. He sold NeXT to Apple for $427 million where it evolved into the Mac OS X, the backbone of the new era of Apple. Today, anticipating Apple's latest release generates lines around the block for hours, if not days.

Eight years later in 2005, Apple Inc was one of the most successful comeback stories in corporate history with its desktop computers, laptops and iPods (the iPhone and iPad were yet to come). Steve was asked to address the Stanford University graduation class. A college dropout himself from Oregon's Reed College in 1972, Steve gave the graduates three simple stories from his life:

1. He revealed how he had been adopted and that his birth mother had made his adoptive parents promise they would send him to college. But when he saw his parents' sacrifice, spending most of their savings on a private college, he couldn't bear it. He dropped out, slept on friends' couches, collected soda cans and

attended courses he would have otherwise never have enjoyed – like calligraphy. If he hadn't been open to his own curiosity, the Macintosh might never have offered the beautiful range of fonts that made Apple the pioneer in desktop publishing.

2. Steve mentioned that he had recently been diagnosed with pancreatic cancer. His near brush with death – at that time – taught him to look in the mirror every morning, and ask himself, 'Do I really want to be doing this?' And if too many days passed when he didn't like what he was doing, he changed course.

3. He reminded the graduates that he came from a pre-computer/internet era when ideas were shared in mimeographed, makeshift magazines like the once-beloved *Whole Earth* Catalogue. On the back page of the last-ever issue, there was a photo of a lone country road, a dirt path into an infinite horizon. Beneath it, one line: 'Stay hungry. Stay foolish.' Steve's final advice to the graduates was this: stay open, stay curious. You never know where life will lead you. He said that he had just trusted 'it would all work out'. He was vulnerable, self-deprecating, funny – even humble.

But perhaps Steve's greatest, most visionary speech was his very last one on 7 June, 2011. To everyone's surprise, he appeared at the Cupertino City Council meeting in California to appeal for support as Apple planned to build their first headquarters, housing 12,000+ employees, on the grounds of former asphalt parking lots once owned by Hewlett-Packard. By this time, it was well known that Steve was battling terminal pancreatic cancer. Though he was still CEO of Apple, no one would have faulted him if he had not appeared for this Monday night meeting. Surely, Tim Cook (his eventual replacement as chairman and CEO) or Jonathan Ive (chief design officer), could have taken it.

But this was personal to Steve. A frisson of energy crackled across the room – the crowd whooped and applauded as a very thin and frail Steve Jobs stood up to face the Cupertino City Council. He wanted to share his vision for the eventual world headquarters for Apple Inc. He said, 'We went out and bought some land, about 150 acres, once owned by Hewlett-Packard. And this land is kind of special to me.' Clicking through his Keynote presentation, Steve revealed an awe-inspiring circular spaceship of a building surrounded by trees – and with apricot orchards in the centre. The HQ circle would be entirely made of curved glass (not the cheapest thing to do). The architect's design looked like the Mother Ship had just landed.

Steve spoke of his love for this particular plot of land. 'Hewlett and Packard were my idols,' he said, revealing that when he was 13 years old, he called Bill Hewlett on his home phone, adding, 'This gives you an idea of my age, because all phone numbers were listed at that time.' Steve asked Bill for spare parts for a project he was building, a frequency counter. Bill gave him the parts, but he did something far more important. He gave Steve a job that summer. Steve said he was 'in heaven' going to work at Hewlett-Packard every day.

He spoke of his childhood love of walking amongst the apricot groves that were once ubiquitous, now mostly cut down. So, he hired a world-class arborist from Stanford University because he wanted this campus to be filled with trees indigenous to the region once again. He emphasized that they were creating a building entirely off the grid, with their own natural gas energy and biodiesel fueled buses. When asked about the air quality within the building, Steve said, 'Both of my parents died of lung cancer. So I'm a little sensitive on that topic.' In every question posed to him, Steve made it personal: his childhood heroes, his love of the region, his passion for green spaces, his remembrance of his parents. Finally, a councillor asked him what, perhaps, Apple might give back to the community, free wifi for example. Steve calmly took the upper hand and said, 'As you know, we're the largest taxpayer in Cupertino, so we're continuing to stay here and pay taxes. Because if we can't, we take our people and go to Mountain View.' (Apple is one of the most profitable corporations in the world). He continued, 'I'm a simpleton. We pay taxes, and I believe the city should do those things. Now, if we can get out of paying taxes, I'll be glad to put up wifi.' Ouch!

He then shifted back to the purpose of his coming: his full belief in the future of his company, 'I think we do have a shot at building the best office complex in the world. I really do believe that architecture students would come here to see this, for years to come. I really do believe it could be that good.' He concluded by saying, 'We want to break ground next year. And we want to move in by 2015.' At the meeting's end, all the councillors thanked Steve for being the 'hometown boy' he was – that he had grown up there, graduated from Homestead High School, and was now giving so much back. Steve left the meeting quietly, saying simply, 'Thank you very much.'

Two months later, on 24 August, he resigned as CEO. He continued to work as chairman until the day before he died on 5 October. The world mourned with candle-lit vigils and mountains of flowers, bit-into apples and old

Macs lining the front of Apple stores. At Steve's memorial service at Apple's headquarters, former vice president, Al Gore, an Apple board member, quoted the Beatles in homage to Steve, saying, 'In the end, the love you take is equal to the love you make.'

In 2017, Sir Jonathan Ive stood in the midst of the finally ready Apple headquarters in Cupertino, California. The Stanford University arborist had successfully overseen the planting of hundreds of indigenous trees, including the restoration of Steve's beloved apricot groves. The Apple HQ campus was, at long last, opening its doors to the world, and – within their state-of-the-art Steve Jobs Theatre – Tim Cook proudly introduced the new future of Apple: the iPhone X. Surveying the exquisite building materials – the white oak doors and furnishings, polished concrete floors and the curved glass walls encompassing the great circle that will house Apple's 12,000+ employees, Jony Ive said simply, 'What I was not prepared for, was how much the glass reflects all this green. Into infinity.'

Applying the Tools of Storytelling

Gleaming Detail

Look at how Steve always speaks with a 'long view'. In his first speech to the Stanford University graduates, he imparts three stories: his birth mother's request that his adoptive parents send him to college; his brush with death and renewed focus on the Now; and his own life philosophy for how to live well. He leaves the students with a Gleaming Detail – a clear image of the photograph of a simple dusty road leading to the lone horizon. He concludes by urging them to 'Stay hungry, stay foolish.'

Know what your audience wants and needs to hear

Notice that all of Steve's concepts are universal: birth, parents, college, death, an unknown future. They relate personally to the audience he is speaking to on this day: university graduates. It's what they care about. He speaks to their fear and to their *wonder*. It would be fair, I think, to presume that if he were speaking to a gathering of Fortune 500 billionaires, he would have chosen three other stories, personal to him while universal in their shared life experiences.

Dare to be vulnerable

Steve revealed to the world several personal – possibly very private – moments: that he was adopted, that he dropped out of college and was broke, and that he had been diagnosed with cancer (this created international headline news). Steve dared to share his own story; in so doing, he connected not only with his audience, but the entire world. This speech is consistently ranked as one of the top five university graduation speeches of all time.

Juxtaposition

Consider Steve's 'Think different' advertisement, which begins, 'Here's to the crazy ones, the misfits and rebels...' These words, 'negative verbal slurs', vividly contrast with the black-and-white images of the visionaries who helped define the 20th century: from Einstein to Gandhi to John Lennon. This is storytelling at its purest – show, don't tell. Steve's commercial dares the viewing audience into a state of *wonder*. You pause and ruminate about what it took for each of these people to change the world. The conclusion: if you dare to 'think different', you might well change the world, too. You might also dare to buy an Apple computer.

Evoke the senses

In chapter 7, the Five Senses are presented as a way to focus your storytelling. But Steve's storytelling comes from a deeper sense – which I will now call the Sixth Sense – *wonder*. In his talk to the Cupertino City Council, Steve begins with his love of his childhood heroes, Hewlett and Packard, who were the original pioneers of the computer era. They too built a world-class company from within this small community. Bill Hewlett gave Steve his first summer job, which Steve recalls as 'heaven'. Steve speaks of the 'wonder' of that time in his life, how, as a boy, he walked through the apricot orchards, and now the wonder of Apple being able to build their first corporate headquarters on HP's very same land.

Hand over the spark

Even as Steve – facing his own mortality – regales the City Council with his vision for Apple's new headquarters, he never stops speaking of the future. With every question they ask, he reframes the question to his personal vision:

when asked about air and safety standards, Steve could have replied with a standard corporate answer. Instead, Steve replies – with elevated urgency – 'That question is extremely personal to me. Both my parents died of lung cancer.' Again, he takes the 'long view' – his parents' untimely deaths have transformed how he will insure the future health of Apple's employees.

Steve casts his final 'long view' vision for the City Council and the world, saying, 'I believe Apple has the chance to create a world-class building that someday architect students from all over the world will come to visit.' Steve speaks about the future with comfort, as if he already lives there.

Exercises

1. How do you feel upon reading this story?

2. Has a state of wonder been evoked? And if so, how might you envision the future?

3. When you tell your story, think of the direct wants and concerns of your audience. What do they need to hear from you? How can you 'hand over your spark'?

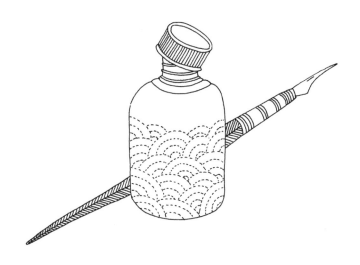

'The unexamined life is not worth living.'

—

Socrates

10
So, What's Your Story?

So often, simply telling a story can be a healing act. You discover clarity purely by expressing what has happened. Confusion dissipates. This is why we report events to each other. Why we're asked, 'What happened?' What has always amazed me is that no matter what the event, whether good or bad, the first question asked by any well-meaning reporter is, 'How do you feel?' To which the standard response is so often, 'I can't ... I don't have the words.' We are all seeking emotional clarity when we tell a story.

To reveal how universal a story can be, in every class I teach, I always start my students with three exercises.

The first is to consider where you were when a major event occurred. More importantly, try to focus on exactly what you were doing when you understood what was happening.

When you do this exercise, think about your 'hook' or 'lead' that sets up the story with a modicum of context. We need just enough information to explain that this story is important. That is, provide the GPS to situate your audience: the place, time and era.

This initial setup should be in direct contrast to the

ending – the punchline, if you will – of your story. You'll remember we discussed the idea of juxtaposition – introducing at the beginning the opposite idea to the ending. These two opposing ideas in your story will collide to create a whole new idea. This collision of ideas adds impact and will incite your audience to ruminate long after the story has ended.

Let's take 11 September 2001. For the first few years after this world-changing event, wherever I travelled in the world, I began my lecture series by asking my students to share what they were doing on that day when they realised what was happening. Consider doing this yourself, now, by sharing your experience with someone close to you or by writing about this day in your journal or notebook.

Throughout the world, my experience has been that the room hushes as thick memories blanket each student. And, sure enough, each student's recollection begins with an ordinary moment – usually a sound – when they were 'awakened' by the news. Many were asleep, of course, when the phone rang, or someone pounded on the door, or they heard a roommate shout in horror. But next, they all recall – as if in passing – what a beautiful fine blue day it was, regardless of where they were living at the time. It's as if the perfection of that late summer day made the shock of the events that followed all the worse.

There are too many stories to tell, of course, around this particular date and you'll have your own. Maybe you don't even want to go there. But I want to tell you the following two stories to reveal how powerful and direct a memorable event can be.

Bill was producing a student film, in a boat on the water off Long Island, which so happened to have a view of the World Trade Center towers. The students were laughing and shouting when Bill heard a gasp. The boat's captain was looking up and off towards the World Trade Center just as the plane entered the first tower. Vivid red flames gushed out the other side of the tower. Bill had worked on those floors, as an intern, just that summer at Cantor Fitzgerald, where his uncle and cousin now worked. He knew all the people on those floors. He had walked those very halls. The captain turned off the engine motor. The boat stilled, just rocking back and forth, as the film crew gaped, in silence. All they could hear were the seagulls calling. When the next plane barrelled into the second tower, everyone cried out, 'NO!' Then, again, they clapped their hands over their mouths. Silent. Just the birds above called. The water lapped. They stood witness, as each tower fell. Then – both times – after viewing the tower's collapse, moments later there came the 'falling sound' roaring out to them in wave upon wave, billowing, until it covered them, too.

Meanwhile, on the other side of the world, a lovely tall woman from Russia, Lena, recalled that she and her friends had gone for a picnic at a remote lake on that same date. They had been skinny-dipping, sun-bathing, and had an old 1950s portable transistor radio playing 'golden oldie' pop music on their picnic table. It was late in the day but still warm as they languished in the late summer evening light. Relaxing with drinks and laughter, suddenly a stern radio announcer interrupted the music with the words, 'The New York City World Trade Centers have been hit by passenger planes and collapsed in a terrorist attack.'

No one could speak or look at each other. Lena's voice caught, as she said, 'It was as if it was the end to all our summers.'

Pause. Consider. How does this make you feel? The power of this story is in letting it go and just allowing it to connect with the audience.

The second exercise I give my students takes them from the universal experience to the deeply personal, even vulnerable. Nobody, of course, wants to go here publicly, But, in fact, the greatest storytellers are willing to reveal themselves 'warts and all'.

As an example, by way of encouragement to get you to share a more personal story, let me tell you one of mine.

Living in Hollywood, I find myself surrounded by ongoing interviews with the leading actresses of the day (and they are always changing). During one Oscar season (the lead-up to the Academy Awards), several Best Actress and Supporting Actress contenders were interviewed by *The Hollywood Reporter*: Anne Hathaway, Sally Field, Naomi Watts, Scarlett Johansson, Helen Hunt and Marion Cotillard – all of whom are considered great beauties and hugely successful.

What followed was, unfortunately, all too typical: they started by revealing some of their worst moments. Anne Hathaway described the humiliation of being universally panned for her hosting of the Academy Awards in 2011; Sally Field gave a humiliating account of needing to do a screen test for Steven Spielberg because she was considered too old for the role of Mary Lincoln (in *Lincoln*). All the other actresses listened sympathetically to Sally's need to still audition despite her 40-year, double-Oscar career.

I thought, I can't imagine any gathering of Best Actor contenders ending with any of the men mentioning humiliating moments. They might share some self-deprecating stories, and laugh among themselves, but they would never have revealed such negative vulnerability.

I read a statistic somewhere a long time ago that had deduced this fact: there are only on average about 12 women in the world, at any given time, deemed the major beauties of our day by the fashion cognoscenti, *Vogue*, *Harper's*, *Elle*, etc. The editors and leading fashion houses rely on the scarcity of the 'star power' of these current beauties to sell their magazines and their products. The net result consigns the rest of us mere mortals to the purgatory of inadequacy and endless comparisons. But here in this Oscar gathering, these beauty superstars felt the need to confess their fears – when they didn't even need to! This led me to ponder, again, why is it women dwell in self-doubt, no matter what their beauty and status?

For two months of every year for over a decade, I taught in Paris at La Fémis – France's most elite film school. Each year, I endured the sight of all the svelte beauties sauntering along the wide boulevards. How do they do it, the French? Even French women in their eighties or nineties are soignée, chic, forever slender as a reed.

And so, every year I would return to Paris to lecture just in time for the annual July sales, which would also mean an annual assault on my self-esteem. 'Why did I not lose those 20 – 30 – 40(!) pounds before I got here! Yet again?!' I'd gnash my teeth, don sackcloth and ashes, even lie prostrate before the god of self-denial, all to change my voluptuous (or, shall I say, voluminous) shape. Always to no avail.

My daily subway route to La Fémis in Montmartre meant I took Metro Line 4 to the 18th arrondissement. My stop was Marchés Barbès, the French–African emigrant centre of Paris – also affectionately known as Paname (slang for 'exotic Paris') – that has a lively outdoor market.

Always, along the route, I would see fantastic African women wearing spectacular, vibrant-patterned, statuesque headdresses. Their muumuu-style sheaths would either match or contrast their headdresses with miles-wide yardage. Babies would be strapped on their backs with even more contrasting coloured-pattern slings. All this captured a seemingly vast, visual space of competing colours, shapes and patterns that seemed to shout, 'Celebrate life!'

Each day, when I came up the Metro steps and walked towards the film school in my neutral beige or black summer dresses, I would pass by a group of these wild-clothed women chattering at the entrance to the market. I would nod and move on but would never engage in conversation – I didn't know their language, nor, probably, did they know mine. Then one day as I came out of the Metro, I bumped into a co-worker from La Fémis, an elegant black Parisian woman. We passed by the group of women. They spoke quickly, overlapping each other, nodding their heads in acknowledgement, as women do all over the world.

My friend and I climbed up the long hill on this hot day towards La Fémis at the top of Montmartre, chatting about nothing in particular. But when we reached her office, she turned to me and said, 'Do you know that those women were speaking about you as we passed them by the Metro?'

'No, I didn't,' I replied.

She said, 'They were saying that you were the most beautiful white woman they had ever seen, because,' she looked me in the eye, 'you have the body of an African.'

So why was this story significant enough for me to tell it here? For starters, I felt my mind fall open to a whole new continent of values. I was humbled. I felt known and, in fact, loved by unseen forces. This was a restoring moment to me. My heart opened. So, yes, this became a big step on my road to self-love ... along with compassion for others.

From then on, I decided to live in the realm of well-being. To choose colour, vibrancy, and to celebrate life more. Now, I make a point of enjoying a great meal two or three times a month. I decided to speak words of appreciation to myself. This action was – and still is – very difficult. To not express any self-loathing, or act with self-doubt, requires a sea change of consciousness.

The third, and most important, exercise I assign my students to help them elevate their storytelling skills is the hardest one. It is also the one they most resist, but soon it becomes the assignment for which they *all* seem to thank me personally. I ask them:

Write about someone who changed your life.

This would be someone significant – perhaps a coach, boss, teacher, friend, lover, and so on. This person could have been mean, a tyrant even, or someone kind, inspirational, loving. Or they may have broken your heart. In my vernacular in cinematic storytelling, I call this character 'the Antagonist' – in your story you are the Protagonist. It's an individual who enters your life and, afterwards, you are never quite the same. The key to this exercise is that you take a 'fearless moral inventory' (to quote our friends in Alcoholics Anonymous) of who you were before this person came into your life – and how you were forever changed thereafter.

All cinematic storytelling is about this one event in the Protagonist's life. It requires, necessitates even, becoming open and vulnerable. Movies elongate and heighten this moment in a two-hour-long journey, one in which we see the Protagonist reluctantly encounter the Antagonist and resist change. But, by the end, the Protagonist has either discovered the courage to become their best self (in drama or comedy), or they have lost the world (in tragedy).

Every year when I give this exercise to my high-achieving students, several in their twenties or early thirties will confidently take me aside to tell me that they have never had an Antagonist in their lives. I will ask if their hearts were ever broken? No, they say. I'll offer, 'Did you ever have a coach, or teacher or minister, even, who changed you?' Usually, they shake their heads. A few may suddenly recall an event, such as a car accident, or their obsession with a great musician, or something external that has changed their outlook. I don't back down. I tell them the assignment is to write about a character, a true Force of Nature in their lives. I also smile to myself because it is simply not possible for these elite students – who have come this far in their lives – not to have encountered an Antagonist. They cajole, prevaricate. Nevertheless, I tell them they have to find a way to complete the exercise.

And, always, they do. They want to explore this area of their lives. They want the insight. But they simply have never allowed themselves to take a 'fearless moral inventory', to become vulnerable, to consider that they would even need to change. We all need to change. This is at the very core of storytelling: we discover who we are.

What is interesting here is that my students – after all their resistance or seeming diffidence – end up discovering something new about themselves by looking deep within. They uncover, and then want to tell, stories of exceptional verve, heartbreak or courage under pressure. These have been tragedies where coaches misused their world-class sports talent, parents deceived them in order to pay their taxes, or they found themselves embroiled in an international kidnapping incident in Australia, or they witnessed a student who stood up to the tanks in Beijing, or they have been victims of horrific sexual abuse. But also triumphant tales about great love found at long last. The stories are all extraordinary. Why anyone would not value their own life experience baffles me.

One last thing: once the stories are told in the room, there is always a hush, an awe. Followed by, curiously, an ineffable feeling of 'lightness of being'. My role has only been to lead them on this journey.

So, for this exercise:

1. Ponder: who has been a Force of Nature in your life? Who provoked, incited or caused you to become your best self, even if you loathed them in the process or they broke your heart?

2. What were you like before? Name your fear. Isolate an example of that fear, an inaction that pole-axed you.

3. Isolate a 'gleaming detail' – an ordinary moment that becomes extraordinary upon reflection.

4. Is there a prevailing sense memory specific to this story?

5. What is the GPS: time, place, context?

6. What happened? What did the Antagonist do – or not do – that provoked you to conscious change? Note, I say 'conscious change'.

7. What action did you take to change? Usually it is an ordinary moment. Focus on this. Maybe it's the time you gave up your sport out of frustration, fear or sense of failure. But at this moment, you walk back on to the court and play. Again. This time with renewed resolve, joy or maturity. The point is that you are a changed person, and this is the story we want to hear.

8. Don't describe the change. Tell the change with an action moment, or a contrasting moment or a twist on the event.

'The universe is made of stories, not of atoms.'

—

Muriel Rukeyser

11
Why We Need Stories

Stories are, at heart, like the baton handed over in a relay team, only they are passed from one generation to the next. They give each of us a visual template of what to expect, a map of the 'wilderness', but most of all the best stories provide a sort of psychological preparation for life's inevitable struggles. In short, stories are prescriptions for courage. They illustrate how to run the race. And win. We are not born with courage. We may possess bravado, even arrogance. Youth normally does. But courage is a quiet, spiritual muscle discovered only when you face your greatest fear. Stories embolden, strengthen, and establish how we can become our very best. No one better understood this than Winston Churchill.

In the 1930s, known as his 'Wilderness Years', where he was marginalised in Parliament, and viewed as an antiquated Victorian-era warrior with a seemingly outsized (even for the British) love of champagne, brandy and cigars, Winston Churchill stood notably apart. He, alone, warned of Hitler's growing menace to Europe and Great Britain. In 1938, Britain's then prime minister, Neville Chamberlain, sought appeasement with Hitler, and came home smiling, waving their negotiated Munich Agreement. Of course, Hitler never meant any of it. He ordered the Nazi army to invade Poland in 1939, and Britain was forced to declare war on Germany for the second time in 25 years, on 3 September 1939. Undeterred, the Nazis continued their ruthless rampage, with their Panzer tanks ploughing over Poland's paltry horse-led cavalry, marauding across Belgium and Holland's flimsy farmers' fields, even blasting through France's Maginot Line with a might such as had never before been imagined. They invaded and conquered with ease. Each country fell, within days, until only Great Britain remained – an island apart – the one last, small realm ready to topple. But the worst of times have a way of raising up a true leader. On 10 May 1940, Chamberlain tendered his resignation to King George VI, recommending Winston Churchill as the next prime minister.

On 13 May, he prepared to address the House of Commons for the first time as prime minister. Churchill – who would say later, 'The British are the only people who like to be told bad news' – spoke gravely, humbly and frankly: 'I have nothing to offer but blood, toil, tears and sweat ... You ask, what is our policy? I will say: it is to wage war, by sea, land and air, with all our might. You ask, what is our aim? I can answer in one word: victory. Victory at all costs, victory in spite of all terror, victory, however long and hard the road may be.'

You could say that Churchill somehow knew the story he was acting in, and was telling his people how it would end.

If ever there was a person who understood the context of his times it was Churchill. From that day on, for 19 lone months – while the US remained staunch in their 'neutral' stance – Britain faced the onslaught of Hitler's Nazi fury.

And early in his premiership, they had endured the bitter pill of the Battle of France, when France fell to the

Nazis in May 1940. The British, French and Belgian troops were forced to retreat, and 338,000 men found themselves stranded on the beaches of Dunkirk in northern France, at the English Channel.

Churchill called it a 'colossal military disaster', declaring that 'The whole root and core and brain of the British Army' would either be captured or perish once the Nazis resumed their offensive. But, for some mysterious reason, Hitler failed to press home his attack. Thus, between 27 May and 4 June 1940, a hastily assembled armada of 850 boats – from British destroyers to small merchant marine, fishing boats, lifeboats and pleasure craft – sailed to and from Dunkirk for nine days. They ferried these 338,000 men back to Britain, in an event that became known as the Miracle of Dunkirk. However, the British army had been forced to leave all their armour and equipment behind.

That night, 4 June, now that all the men were safely on British soil, Churchill addressed the House of Commons:

'We shall not flag or fail. We shall go on to the end ... We shall defend our island, whatever the cost may be. We shall fight on the beaches, we shall fight on the landing-grounds, we shall fight in the fields and in the streets, we shall fight in the hills. We shall never surrender.'

All of Great Britain knew that Hitler's invasion would soon begin. The tension was palpable, almost unbearable in the waiting. The race to rearm was furiously upon them.

Churchill's daily schedule became the stuff of legend. Now, though he was in his mid-sixties and had been a heavy drinker all his life, he seemed to have indomitable energy. He slept in small naps, always supped a full bottle of champagne through the day, and chomped through countless cigars. In the evening, he turned to brandy and would listen to British military music on long-playing records. When he 'got the rhythm' of his thinking right, several secretaries would be called – at all hours of the day or night – ready to write down his words. He would pace, speak out loud, call for the typewritten version from their shorthand, and edit and polish his speeches through the early hours.

Thus, on 18 June, Churchill spoke again in the House of Commons, and repeated the speech on BBC radio in the evening: 'The Battle of France is now over, and the Battle of Britain is about to begin. Upon this battle depends the survival of Christian civilisation. Upon it depends our own British life, and our Empire. Hitler knows that he will have to break us in this island or lose the war. If we can stand up to him, all Europe may be free and the life of the world may move forward into broad, sunlit uplands. But if we fall, then the whole world, including the United States, including all that we have known and cared for, will sink into the abyss of a new Dark Age made more sinister, and perhaps more protracted, by the lights of perverted science. Let us therefore brace ourselves to our duties, and so bear ourselves that, if the British Empire and its Commonwealth lasts for a thousand years, men will still say, "This was their finest hour!"'

No one knew then what we know now – about Hitler's eventual 'Final Solution plan' to create concentration camps, his systematically organised genocide that was to come. How did Churchill have this prescience? And so the Battle of Britain began. Hitler ordered the entire might of the Luftwaffe to fly across the Channel, daily, throughout the summer of 1940. To Hitler's shock the Royal Air Force fought back, ably prepared with Spitfires and Hurricanes, ready to fly high for the dogfights into the fine, blue skies. Young men, like 'knights of old', as Churchill proclaimed, jousted in the skies, holding back the entire Luftwaffe. Churchill declared, 'Never in the field of human conflict has so much been owed by so many to so few.' Furious at this continuing stalemate, Hitler ordered the night-time Blitz (German for 'lightning') of London, throughout the autumn of 1940. In terrifying formation, the Luftwaffe rained down bombs, killing thousands of civilians. Fires devoured central London.

And, whenever the BBC could record Churchill, the entire British Empire, it seemed, would gather to listen to his speeches on the wireless.

Looking on, from high atop London's rooftops, Edward R. Murrow, the first great US radio journalist, reported back to the States, saying, 'Churchill mobilized the English language and sent it into battle.'

A rare and even witty courage shone forth out of the British. While the East End of London burned to the ground, sirens hurried the British into the tube stations doubling as makeshift air-raid shelters. Once the 'all clear' was sounded after the night raids, someone would call out for a cuppa, or jeer, 'Is that all you got, Jerry?!'

Where had they found this pluck?

Throughout his life, Churchill had endured several 'wilderness periods': he'd had a very lonely childhood at his family's grand estate at Blenheim Palace, ignored by his profligate parents. In his solitude, he had devoured history, concentrating on Edward Gibbon's eight-volume *History of the Decline and Fall of the Roman Empire*, MacAulay's 12-volume *History of England*, as well as a hundred volumes of the *British Annual Register*.

This is where Churchill gained his depth, strength and vision – by studying stories of old, stories of courage under fire, portraits of character revealed under pressure, tales of resilience or failure – all of them true stories gleaned from history. This vast backlog of human endeavour is what

Churchill handed on to his beleaguered nation during the dark, depressing days of 1940–41. Churchill had so dined, for years, on history – what it takes to survive, thrive and win – until, as Isaiah Berlin the Oxford philosopher wrote, Churchill imposed his 'will and imagination upon his countrymen ... with such intensity that in the end they approached his ideals and began to see themselves as he saw them'.

Still, by the late autumn of 1941, after 18 months of this relentless aggression, there appeared to be no end in sight. Privately, he confessed that he was suffering a terrible depression. On 29 October 1941, Churchill went to Harrow School to listen to some traditional songs for inspiration. While there, he was asked if he would give the students a speech.

He rose and said the following:

'Surely, what we have gone through in this period – I am addressing myself to the School – surely from this period of ten months, this is the lesson: Never give in, never give in, never, never, never, never – in nothing, great or small, large or petty – never give in, except to convictions of honour and good sense. Never yield to force; never yield to the apparently overwhelming might of the enemy.'

Six weeks later, on 7 December 1941, the Japanese bombed Pearl Harbor, and the United States entered the war. The rest, as they say, is history. Three and a half years on, a defeated Hitler committed suicide and on 8 May 1945, Germany signed the 'unconditional surrender'.

All over the world – the British Empire, the US, Europe – everyone gathered at their radio to listen to Churchill announce: 'The war in Europe is now over.'

Churchill gave Britain and the world a vision of where relentless wit, courage and determination can lead you.

Stories, told well and acted upon by one generation, ignite the next generation to greatness: because they have heard with their own ears, and seen with their own eyes, what courage can achieve, namely that each individual, emboldened, strengthened and established in their own courage, passes this on to another – like a great Olympic relay race. This was how the war was won. And now, the generations following on later have Churchill to thank for his passion for story. As my father, a Churchill scholar and historian, told me over and over again from the day I was born, 'Churchill was the twentieth century's indispensable man.'

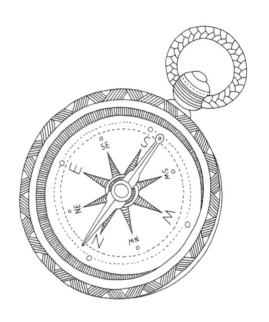

'We shall not cease from all our exploration.
And the end of all our exploring
will be to arrive where we started
and know the place for the first time.'

—

T.S. Eliot

Conclusion

Why did I choose to share the stories that I did?
About activists, visionaries, leaders, entrepreneurs?

What all great stories have in common is a journey
whose conclusion appears uncertain. They are full of
hope. And they are about courage. The tragic ones are
about someone who did not have the courage to do
something they had to do, or who took the coward's
way out.

This is how we connect to our humanity, and become
better people. How well you tell your story can make the
difference to anything you do – whether that's convincing
someone to love you, buy something you've made, or give
something of themselves; or how well you make your way
in the world; or, simply, in sharing who you are.

I have realised that in writing this book, I have simply
enjoyed sharing the stories of my heroes – the world
famous and those known only to a relative few. But the
greater stories, to me, may well be the personal ones told
by my students, each one of them unique, emotional
and memorable. This, in part, is because I had the great
pleasure of observing them as they all learned to tell
these stories, and to tell them well. Storytelling is native

to all of us. We just need to do it. Dare to be personal. Dare to be vulnerable. And dare to listen to others sharing their stories.

And, why should you do this? Risk your vulnerability? Because in this age of content creation, someone is telling a story all the time. In fact, we are immersed in them, and even make life choices because of them. Thus, it is necessary for us to harness our own stories, and tell them well. If not, then someone else will come in and wallpaper our culture with their stories. And then, how do we pass on to the next generation what has been lost, if not forgotten?

Remember Churchill: never, ever forget.

In the end, all you have is your story.

Tell us your story.

Do.

Exercises

The following are exercises for you to practise. We've come across some of them earlier in the book, and here they are collected so you can work through them. First write down your story – in a journal, on scraps of paper, on your computer, it doesn't matter – then try speaking it out loud. If you can't find a sympathetic friend or family member to listen to it, just talk to the mirror. As well as allowing you to try out the things discussed in the book, you might want to stockpile a few of these as they can be helpful to you in conversational settings. Before you start, here are a few things to remember:

— In the words of Lionel Logue in *The King's Speech*, 'Just speak to me, as a friend.'
— Be short, be concise. Try not to take more than five to seven minutes for each exercise.
— Never play the victim. Always reveal an action you took or reveal how you changed later upon reflection.
— Be specific. Choose visual examples.
— Remember the five senses and try to evoke one sense memory specific to each story.
— Make sure your story has a beginning, middle and end.
— Leave your audience wanting more.
— Above all, observe how your audience is listening and adapt accordingly.

Exercise 1
Tell us something about yourself we wouldn't otherwise know.
Remember: humility and humour go a long, long way.
Yes, you're the centre of attention. But you have to forget about that. Surrender your ego. This is a great gesture on your part: to reveal yourself to others, in a way that explains who you are, and yet also gives them an insider's understanding of a world they would otherwise never know.

Exercise 2
Try and recall a favourite childhood story.
Something the family always told about you, or you told about yourself.

Exercise 3
Tell us about an antagonist or 'force of nature' person in your life.
They could be a teacher, mentor, coach, clergyman, boss, family friend, some older influence in your life – for good or bad (and see page 105).

Exercise 4
Tell us about the first time your heart was broken.
It could be when you were 5, 15, 25, or last week. Try to make this humorous. What absurd or crazy thing did you do? The key thing here is to describe the person briefly. Share something great about that person however small it may seem (remember, the more ordinary the detail, the more universal it will become); then describe the break-up

or the moment your heart was broken. Again, describe the ordinary moment, recall the sense memory that intensified for you at that moment. There's always one. Then, describe the action you took to heal, recover or move on. Expand that moment – give us the action reveal. Avoid saying, 'And then I realised ...' Or, 'Later ...' Take us into the vulnerable place. We all have been there. We want to go into that place with you – again. But the take-away should be how you were changed by this, or rose above it.

Exercise 5
How were you affected by a seminal cultural or sporting event?
Something like the Olympics, a Royal Wedding, Live Aid, or your team winning the FA Cup.

Exercise 6
Share a 'Cusp of an Era' event.
It could be graduation from college or a wedding (yours or a significant other), when you left home, or the day you became a mother or father.

Exercise 7
Tell us about a powerful, major event that many of us shared.
Where were you and what were you doing when Princess Diana died, when Kurt Cobain committed suicide, or the day of the 9/11 attack on the Twin Towers, for example?

Exercise 8

Can you recall a small event that moved you or changed you?

This could be anything: the YouTube clip of a deaf girl hearing for the first time; the photo of the NYC cop buying shoes and socks for a homeless man with bare feet in terribly cold weather; or something much more personal like witnessing an elderly family member fight impending Alzheimer's by listening very hard and then writing everything down as you said it.

Exercise 9

Sell us on an idea of yours, or a cause that you really care about.

The key here is to not finger-wag, rant or preach, or take a self-righteous or snide tone. Rather:

— Share your idea as a possibility to consider.
— Come up with a gleaming detail, an image.
— 'Hand over the spark' – relay a small scenario that explains your passion.
— Most importantly, how has this changed you? Why do you care so much?

Exercise 10

What is a passion of yours, and why?

Be specific. For example, why do you love movies, or surfing, rock-climbing, watching football / golf / tennis, baking bread or gardening? Ask yourself the following questions:

— What is it that you love?
— What is it about you that you are revealing?

- When did you first 'fall in love' with this passion?
- What specifically captured your attention, altered your life course forever?
- How has this passion changed your life?
- Where has it led you? Be specific: give a small example, an action moment.
- What sense memory do you recall that relates to this event?
- What was your life before this passion took hold of you and now, how is your life today?
- How would you describe this passion to someone who has never experienced it or has no knowledge of it?

And remember, be kind. Tell your stories with a smile.
Share your passion.
Carry the fire.

'Be amusing, never tell unkind stories;
above all, never tell long ones.'

—

Benjamin Disraeli

About the Author

© Skinner Myers

Bobette Buster grew up in Kentucky, a region renowned for its great storytellers. After graduating, she produced an oral history of the area that is now archived at the Kentucky Museum. She then moved to Hollywood to learn the business of script development.

Her first book, *Do Story*, was followed by *Do Listen* in 2018. She is the writer and producer of feature documentary *Making Waves: The Art of Cinematic Sound* (2019) and several narrative and documentary projects including *Charlotte*, *Generation Nerd Girls* and *The Common Man*. In 2019, she gave a TEDx Lecture entitled *The Radical Act of Storytelling*.

She has been a story consultant and speaker to major studios including Pixar, Disney, Sony Animation and Amazon Games, as well as to leading production companies, non-profits and creative agencies around the world.

Bobette is the visiting lecturer of Science and Storytelling at Tufts University, and continuing guest lecturer of Cinematic Story Development at Milan Catholic University. She lives in Los Angeles, California.

You can connect with Bobette on Twitter: *@bobettebuster* or via her website: *bobettebuster.com*

Thanks

Certainly, I thank God for leading me through the 'valley of the shadow of death' during the long era of the passing of my brothers – Lowell and Charles, the magical ones – when all I could do was teach storytelling. It was in observing the eternal verities of storytelling passed down through the ages that I was able to endure. During this time, I was often led to reflect on a Zen Buddhist saying: 'To master something, you must first learn to teach it.' So I must thank Larry Turman, the Director of the USC Peter Stark Program, for his 'blink' (in the Malcolm Gladwell sense), in seeing in me the teacher I became, but would never have chosen to be.

I thank those who have allowed me to share their stories in this book, especially Scott Harrison, Shan Williams and DJ Forza. And my students the world over for teaching me the inexhaustible power of storytelling. I've always learned far more than them from their endless questions, and new stories told from every aspect of human existence possible.

I have so very many friends and loved ones to thank for gamely listening to my stories, ad infinitum (perhaps ad nauseam), including my beloved Eric and Melissa Ocean, Margie Whitaker, Mark and Rachelle Hutchens, Greg and

Rick Stikeleather, dear friends Gwen Terpstra, M'Leigh
Koziol, Beverly Allen, Matia Karrell, Rebecca Ver Stratten-
McSparren, Roberta Ahmanson, Barbara Nicolosi, Polly
March, Karen Johnson and Andrea McCall. Along with
my 'nieces and nephews' who gave me, their 'crazy aunt',
many a story to tell after so many of our capers: Alex, Jack,
Annie, Laina, Richard Ryan, Madison, Morgan, Gianna
and Philip. I thank Brian and Christabel Eastman for
their many acts of hospitality; along with the many story
compatriots I have met – all from my storytelling travels
including Steve Turner and Beryl Richards in London;
Armando Fumagalli, Marco Alessi, Carla Quarto Di Palo,
Gina Gardini and Francesca Longardi in Italy; Henriette
Buegger in Cologne; Christine Camdessus, Isabel Calle and
Ana Laguna in Ronda; Alain Rocca and Jacqueline Borne
in Paris; Mary Lyons, Sorcha Loughnane, Judy Lunny and
Tricia Perrot in Dublin. And, if I could, I would name all
the 'lovely others' with whom our stories created 'more
memories than the rain …'

Finally, I must thank Miranda West, whose unflagging
determination and charming, wry wit have willed this book
into existence and given me, in the words of Muhammad
Ali, 'last-minute stamina'.

Index

INDEX

Books in the series

Also available

Available in print, digital and audio formats from booksellers or via our website: **thedobook.co**

To hear about events and forthcoming titles, you can find us on social media **@dobookco**, or subscribe to our newsletter